Second Edition

UNDERSTANDING MUSIC FUNDAMENTALS

R. Phyllis Gelineau

Professor of Music
Southern Connecticut State University

PRENTICE HALL, Englewood Cliffs, NJ 07632

Library of Congress Cataloging-in-Publication Data

Gelineau, R. Phyllis.
  Understanding music fundamentals / R. Phyllis Gelineau.—2nd ed.
  p.   cm.
  Includes index.
  ISBN 0-13-928722-1
  1. Music—Theory, Elementary. 2. Music—Handbooks, manuals, etc.
I. Title.
MT7.G3 1992
781—dc20

                  91-28163
                  CIP
                    MN

**To Manson Van B. Jennings—
a dear heart and a gentle person.**

Editorial/production supervision
  and interior design: **Michael R. Steinberg**
Cover design: **Ray Lundgren Graphics, LTD.**
Prepress Buyer: **Herb Klein**
Manufacturing Buyer: **Patrice Fraccio**
Acquisitions Editor: **Bud Therien**

Credits and copyright acknowledgments appear on pp. viii–ix,
which constitute an extension of the copyright page.

 © 1992, 1987 by Prentice-Hall, Inc.
A Simon & Schuster Company
Englewood Cliffs, New Jersey 07632

ISBN 0-13-928722-1

PRENTICE-HALL INTERNATIONAL (UK) LIMITED, *London*
PRENTICE-HALL OF AUSTRALIA PTY. LIMITED, *Sydney*
PRENTICE-HALL CANADA INC., *Toronto*
PRENTICE-HALL HISPANOAMERICANA, S.A., *Mexico*
PRENTICE-HALL OF INDIA PRIVATE LIMITED, *New Delhi*
PRENTICE-HALL OF JAPAN, INC., *Tokyo*
SIMON & SCHUSTER ASIA PTE. LTD., *Singapore*
EDITORA PRENTICE-HALL DO BRASIL, LTDA., *Rio de Janeiro*

Contents

Preface

Individuals who perceive music as being only for the elite and themselves as "non-musical" or having "no talent" can experience deep feelings of anxiety at the outset when facing a music course for the first time. Providing extra support to such learners through simplified explanations and adequate practice materials represents the author's heartfelt attempt to alleviate such anxiety and enhance the learning experience.

This second edition of *Understanding Music Fundamentals*, like its predecessor, is designed to be used by the non-major whose musical needs are assumed to be neither as broad nor as deep as those of the potential professional.

Featured in this edition are additional new songs, more practice materials, sections on transposition, form, phrasing, and musical texture, as well as some modification of the text to facilitate learner progress. The format remains the same:

1. introduction of each new music concept followed by illustrative musical examples;
2. questions and answers on the explanatory material for instant learner feedback;
3. practice essentials for immediate application;
4. experiential activities for reenforcing music concepts.

Vocal and instrumental approaches to the acquisition of music skills have been incorporated throughout and may be used in any desired sequence to permit flexibility in instruction. Instruments included are piano, recorder, Autoharp, harmonica, ukulele, guitar, and selected percussion, accompanied by a broad spectrum of traditional and contemporary song literature for playing and singing.

The *Activities* suggested in various chapters are intended to reenforce the musical learnings under study, encourage maximum participation, and provide opportunities for creative expression.

Acknowledgments

The author is most deeply grateful to all who gave permission to reprint copyrighted and other material. In the case of a few songs, despite sincere and extended efforts, their sources could not be uncovered. If there is a lack of proper acknowledgment in any place, it is only because the source is unknown. The author would very much appreciate being informed about any such instances so that proper acknowledgment can be made and appropriate arrangements secured for any future editions. Special thanks are extended to those sources indicated for permission to use the following:

"African Percussion Ensemble," from *Exploring Music 6*, Teacher's Edition (Holt, Rinehart & Winston, 1975).

"Bill Bailey," from *The Music Book*, Teacher's Edition, Grade 6 by Eunice Boardman, et al., copyright © 1984 by Holt, Rinehart and Winston, Inc., reprinted by permission of the publisher.

"Brother James' Air," from *Music for Young Americans 5* (D.C. Heath, 1963).

"Chopsticks" and "Streets of Laredo," from *Studying Music* (D.C. Heath, 1966).

"Cockles and Mussels," arranged by Buryl A. Red, from *Exploring Music: The Senior Book*, by Beth Landis (Holt, Rinehart & Winston, 1969).

"Consider Yourself," from the Columbia Pictures-Romulus film *Oliver!* Words and music by Lionel Bart. © Copyright 1960 Lakeview Music Co., Ltd., London. TRO-Hollis Music, New York, controls all publication rights for the U.S. and Canada. Used by permission.

Descant for "Streets of Laredo," from *World of Music 5* (Silver Burdett & Ginn, 1988).

"Doo-bee," from *Silver Burdett Music 8* (Silver Burdett, 1982).

"Everybody Loves Saturday Night," from *Exploring Music 6* (Holt, Rinehart & Winston, 1984).

"Good Night, Ladies," from *Silver Burdett Music 7* (Silver Burdett, 1982).

"Gonna Build a Mountain," from the musical production of *Stop the World—I Want to Get Off*. Words and music by Leslie Bricusse and Anthony Newly. © Copyright 1961 TRO Essex Music Ltd., London. TRO Ludlow Music, Inc., New York controls all publication rights for the U.S. and Canada. Used by permission.

"Hallelujah," copyright © 1974 by James Leisy Music from *The Good Times Songbook* by James Leisy. Used by permission of the publisher, Abingdon Press.

"Honey, You Can't Love One," piano accompaniment from *Exploring Music 2*, Teacher's Edition (Holt, Rinehart & Winston, 1975).

"Hush Little Baby," from *Exploring Music 2* (Holt, Rinehart & Winston, 1966).

"I'm Gonna Walk," from *Silver Burdett Music 4* (Silver Burdett, 1981).

"Jesu, Joy of Man's Desiring," from *Singing Together* of OUR SINGING WORLD series, © Copyright 1959, 1957, 1951 by Ginn and Company. Used by permission.

"Kum Ba Yah," words and music by Marvin V. Frey. With African (Angolan) translation. Copyright © 1957, 1958, 1977. Renewed 1985 by Marvin V. Frey. All rights reserved. Used by permission.

"Lavender's Blue," piano accompaniment, from *Exploring Music 2,* Teacher's Edition (Holt, Rinehart and Winston, 1984).

"Let Us Break Bread Together," from *Exploring Music 6* (Holt, Rinehart & Winston, 1966). Reprinted by permission of William S. Haynie.

"No Man Is an Island," from *Songs for Canadian Girl Guides* (Girl Guides of Canada).

"Oh! Susanna," piano accompaniment, from *Exploring Music 2* Teacher's Edition (Holt, Rinehart & Winston, 1971).

"Old Brass Wagon," from *Exploring Music 2* (Holt, Rinehart & Winston, 1984).

"Paddy Works on the Railway," song and countermelody from *World of Music 5* (Silver Burdett & Ginn, 1988).

"Pallet on the Floor," song and countermelody from *World of Music 5* (Silver Burdett & Ginn, 1988).

"Peace Like a River," from *World of Music 3* (Silver Burdett & Ginn, 1988).

"Promised Land," from *Silver Burdett Music 7* (Silver Burdett, 1982).

"Put Your Hand in the Hand," © 1970 by BEECHWOOD MUSIC OF CANADA. U.S. Rights assigned to and controlled by BEECHWOOD MUSIC CORP. Used by permission. Copyright secured. All rights reserved.

"Shalom Alechem," from *The Music Book,* Teacher's Edition, Grade 6 by Eunice Boardman, et al., copyright © 1984 by Holt, Rinehart and Winston, Inc., reprinted by permission of the publisher.

"Short March for Percussion," from *Silver Burdett Music 8* (Silver Burdett, 1976).

"Shoo Fly," from *Exploring Music 2* (Holt, Rinehart & Winston, 1971).

"Sinner Man," from *World of Music 8* (Silver Burdett & Ginn, 1988).

"Trampin'," from *World of Music 5* (Silver Burdett & Ginn, 1988).

Ukulele and piano line drawings, from *Experiences in Music,* by R. Phyllis Gelineau, (McGraw-Hill, 1976)

"Zum Gali Gali," from *World of Music 5* (Silver Burdett & Ginn, 1988).

Chapter One

Elements of Music

Becoming an independent music reader requires an understanding of the signs, symbols, and terms used in music notation and how to translate them into sound. Helping a learner to achieve that understanding is what this book is all about.

Music is made from many different kinds of sounds. A single musical tone, for example, contains the following characteristics: *pitch, duration, intensity,* and *timbre*.

Pitch refers to the *highness* or *lowness* of the tone; *duration* to the *length* of time the tone is sustained; *intensity* to its *loudness* or *softness*; and *timbre* to its *quality*. Timbre is dependent upon the device producing the sound, whether voice, instrument, or other form.

QUESTIONS

1. A single musical tone contains the following characteristics: ___PITCH___, ___INTENSITY___, ___DURATION___ and ___TIMBRE___.

2. ___PITCH___ is the term used when speaking of highness or lowness of a tone.

3. Another word for the loudness or softness of a tone is ___INTENSITY___.

4. The word ___TIMBRE___ refers to the quality of the tone.

Answers p. 285

Most of the songs we hear have a tune and some kind of organized movement that, in musical terms, means they have *melody* and *rhythm*. *Melody* may be defined as "an organized series of tones" or an "arrangement of single tones in a meaningful sequence." Melodies vary widely in character, ranging from the simple—those with a few tones in a limited pitch range—to the more complex—those containing a greater number of tones in extended pitch range. Simple melodies are easier to sing or play, and therefore easier to recall.

Rhythm refers to the *basic pulse* of the music as well as to the series of *long and short sounds* riding over that pulse. Rhythm may also play a part in the setting of a melody. (See Chapters 2 and 3, which both discuss rhythm.)

When a piece of music contains chords produced either vocally or instrumentally, or when two or more compatible melodies are interwoven within the piece, then it may be said to have *harmony*. (See Chapter 9, "Harmony.")

A given musical section may also have a particular kind of structure or design known as *form*. Form is created by various musical devices related to organization and development. (See discussion of form on p. 239.)

Melody, harmony, rhythm, and *form* are often referred to as the *elements of music*. If we are to perceive these elements in a way that will produce the most satisfying aesthetic response, then we must become actively involved in musical experiences such as singing, playing, listening, and creating. It is through such involvement that we may derive not only pleasure and satisfaction but also a deeper knowledge of music and the acquisition of related skills.

QUESTIONS

5. Melody may be defined as _____.
6. Rhythm refers to the _basic_ _pulse_ of the music as well as to the _series of long and short sounds_
7. The elements of music are _melody_, _harmony_, _Rythem_ and _Form_.
8. Structure or design in music is known as _____.
9. The presence of chords and/or interwoven melodies in a given piece of music indicates that it also contains _____.

Answers p. 285

MUSICAL SIGNS AND SYMBOLS

Staff

A staff is a musical symbol upon which music is written. It consists of five horizontal parallel lines and four spaces.

The first line of the staff is on the bottom, the fifth line is on the top. The first space of the staff is on the bottom, the fourth space is on the top.

Fourth space	→ 5th line
Third space	→ 4th line
Second space	→ 3rd line
First space	→ 2nd line
	→ 1st line

QUESTIONS

10. Music is written on a ___Staff___ consisting of ___5___ lines and ___4___ spaces.
11. The bottom line of the staff is the ___1___ line.
12. The top space of the staff is the ___4___ space.

Answers p. 285

Clefs

Every staff has a clef sign at the beginning.

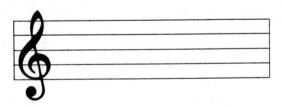

This is a *G* clef 𝄞, sometimes called a *treble* clef.

An acceptable representation of a G or treble clef may be easily made as follows:

1. draw a straight line downward from slightly above the staff to slightly below:

2. draw a curved line to the right, rejoining the first line:

3. extend the curve to the left of the straight line, then circle down and around to the right, rejoining and extending slightly beyond the straight line. Circle back to the left and slightly enclose the second line G:

A slightly fancier version seen in printed music starts with a more curved line and has embellishments on the ends.

There are other clef signs also. This is an *F* clef 𝄢, sometimes called a *bass* clef.

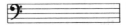

The F or bass clef is simply a right curve followed by two dots that set off the fourth line on this clef:

Draw a few treble and bass clef signs on the staff below:

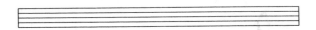

QUESTIONS

13. Where does the clef sign appear? On a staff
14. What sign is this 𝄢? Bass
15. This 𝄞 is the sign of a treble _____ clef.

Answers p. 285

Music written on the treble clef sounds higher when played or sung than music written on the bass clef. Depending on their range, some instruments play from the treble clef, others from the bass clef. When playing the piano with both hands, the left hand usually plays from the bass clef, the right hand from the treble clef.

QUESTIONS

16. Music written on the bass clef sounds (higher, lower) than music written on the treble clef.

17. On the piano the left hand usually plays from the _____ clef.

18. An instrument with a higher range would play from the _____ clef.

Answers p. 285

No matter which clef is used, music written on the *upper* level lines and spaces of the staff will sound *higher* than that written on the lower level lines and spaces; thus the *farther up* the notes ascend on the staff, the *higher* they will sound when played or sung.

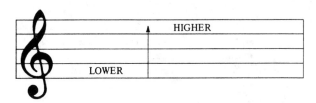

QUESTIONS

19. Music appearing on the upper levels of any given staff will sound _____ than that appearing on the lower levels.

20. A single musical note appearing on the fifth line of the staff will sound _____ (higher, lower) than one appearing on the third space.

Answers p. 285

Letter Names of Staff Lines and Spaces

Every line and space of a staff has a letter name. These letter names refer to different pitch levels according to the clef used. In the *treble* clef the name of the first (bottom) line is *E*; the space immediately above it (first space) is *F*. The letter names then proceed alphabetically through the adjacent lines and spaces. The musical alphabet goes only as far as G, then begins all over again with A:

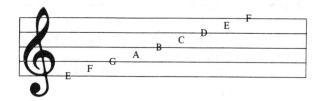

The names of the lines of the treble or G clef are E G B D F:

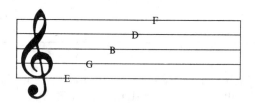

The names of the spaces of the treble or G clef spell FACE:

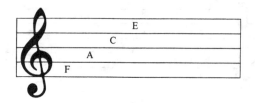

QUESTIONS

21. The musical alphabet does not go beyond the letter
     _____.

22. The first line of the treble clef is _____.

23. The second space of the treble clef is _____.

24. The spaces of the treble clef spell_____.

Answers p. 285

When the bass or F clef is used, the musical alphabet proceeds through the adjacent lines and spaces as it did on the treble clef; however, the name of the first (bottom) line of the bass clef is *G*; thus the corresponding lines and spaces of the bass clef staff will be different from those of the G clef:

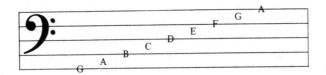

QUESTIONS

25. The bass and treble clefs use the same musical alphabet but begin on different letter names. (True, False)

26. The name of the first space of the bass clef is

    _____.

27. _____ is the last letter of the musical alphabet.

28. *A* is the name of the _____ line of the bass clef.

29. The letters of the second line, third space and third line of the bass clef spell the word _____.

30. The name of the line set off by the two dots next to the F or bass clef is _____.

Answers p. 285

Leger Lines

Sometimes a piece of music requires the use of tones that fall *outside* the range of the five lines of a given staff. When this occurs, lines and spaces may be added above and below the staff through the use of *leger lines*. Leger lines are short lines used to permit the writing of notes above or below a given staff. In the treble clefs shown below, note the use of leger lines for the *ascending* tones G A B C above the staff, and for the *descending* tones C B A G below the staff. In a *descending* progression, the alphabetical order is *reversed*.

When leger lines are used they must be lettered in proper order according to the musical alphabet. When a succession of leger lines is required, each preceding line and space must be accounted for by inserting the appropriate number of lines. In the example below, the note B below middle C shows one line above it (C line), while the G below middle C shows two lines above it (A and C).

QUESTIONS

31. Additional notes may be added above and below the staff through the use of _____ _____.

32. The letter name of the first line *above* the *treble* clef is _____.

33. The letter name of the first line *below* the *treble* clef is _____.

34. When writing a series of leger lines, each previous _____ and _____ must be accounted for.

35. When writing the note G below the treble clef, the leger lines _____ and _____ must be inserted above it.

Answers p. 285

Rules governing the use of leger lines on the treble clef also apply to the bass or F clef. On the bass clefs below note the ascending tones (C D E) and the descending tones (E D C). The *descending* tones are in *reverse alphabetical order,* as they were on the treble clef.

As noted on the treble clef, when writing a series of leger lines, each preceding line and space must be accounted for by inserting the appropriate number of lines.

QUESTIONS

36. A series of leger lines written below a given staff will proceed in _____ alphabetical order.

37. _____ is the letter name for the second line *below* the bass clef.

38. _____ is the letter name for the first line *above* the *bass* clef.

Answers p. 285–286

Great Staff

When the treble and bass clefs are joined, they form the *great* or *grand staff*:

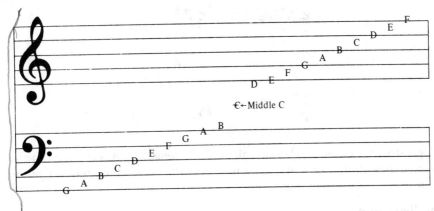

Note that the musical alphabet repeats over and over and that middle C is the dividing point between the two staffs. At one time the middle C line extended the full length of the staff. Today it appears only as a leger line. Whether designated as the first leger line *below* the the treble clef:

or the first leger line *above* the *bass* clef:

it is the same note—middle C—located on the piano directly to the left of two black keys in front of the manufacturer's name.

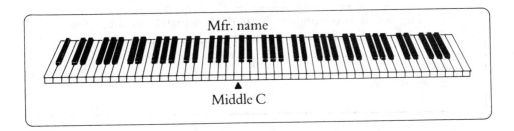

Key Signature

Next to the clef sign on any staff may be found one or more symbols such as these:

♯ = sharp   ♭ = flat.
There may be as many as 7 sharps   or 7 flats

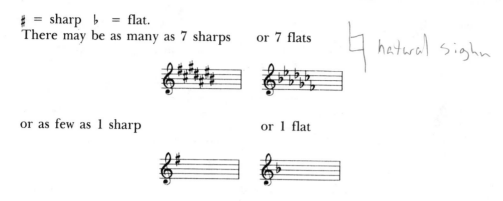

4 hatural sighn

or as few as 1 sharp   or 1 flat

This group of sharps or flats is called a *key signature*. A key signature may contain either sharps or flats. It cannot contain both. If it contains nothing, that in itself is also a key signature.

Time Signature

Immediately to the right of the key signature at the beginning of a piece of music may be found a set of numbers, one over the other. This musical symbol is known as the *meter* or *time signature*. Although the numbers may vary, the location of the meter or time signature remains the same.

QUESTIONS

39. The group of sharps or flats immediately to the right of the clef sign is known as _____ _____.

40. It may contain either _____ or _____.

41. It may also contain _____, which is a _____ _____ as well.

42. The set of two numbers located immediately to the right of the key signature is known as the _____ or _____ _____.

Answers p. 286

In all musical experience, *listening* emerges as the most vitally active and essential ingredient; thus it seems desirable at the outset for learners to engage in activities designed to sharpen listening skills and increase sensitivity to sound—its sources and various qualities. Many of the suggestions shown under Activities below and in other Activities sections throughout this book are intended to achieve this purpose and to provide a path toward deeper involvement and enhanced pleasure.

ACTIVITIES

1. Create different sounds:
    a. using hands in various clapping positions—flat hands, cupped hands, fingertips, backs of the hands, two fingers against the forearm, etc., noting relative pitch differences heard.
    b. striking other parts of the body, such as thighs, knees, or head, with hand.
    c. stamping whole foot, tapping toes, shuffling, etc.

2. Explore possibilities in human vocal sounds (humming, whistling, clicking the tongue, popping, etc.) as well as those made by animals, insects, and other creatures.

3. Explore possible sounds that may be made from manipulation of objects in the immediate environment (books, pens, desks, chairs, etc.).

4. Form groups and create some indoor or outdoor "sound environments" using only nonverbal vocal and body sounds. Have other groups identify the environment.

5. Create a new "machine" combining many different sounds: one person makes a sound and repeats it continuously, another person with a different sound joins in, then another, and so on until the "machine" is complete.

6. Create a sound composition using only vocal and body sounds, with the only requirement being that it have a beginning, middle and end. Sounds may be distributed within each group in any way desired—some solo, some in chorus, etc.

7. Make a non-traditional instrument out of any found object whose sound appeals to you. Form into groups and create compositions using only the "found instruments" (same requirement as for no. 6 above).

8. Tape various sounds from outside the classroom for others to identify. (Random sequences can spark imaginative narration.)

9. Listen to various sounds in the environment—those made by humans and those in nature. Categorize by pitch/no pitch, high/low, loud/soft, long/short, sustained/repeated, rhythmical/non-rhythmical, variable/non-variable, etc.

10. Listen to sounds made by creatures on land, in sea and air: whales, wolves, etc. Categorize as in no. 9 above.

11. Listen to recordings of vocal sounds reflecting lives of people of various cultures, such as vendors, street games, and work calls.

12. Listen to conversation in the language of another culture, noting pitch variation, rhythm and voice inflections.

13. Listen to recordings of musical sounds of various ethnic regions of the world, noting characteristic tone quality and predominant musical elements.

14. Experiment with recorded sounds, using a tape recorder or synthesizer if available.

Chapter Two

Rhythm

Rhythm is everywhere. Night follows day, tides ebb and flow, winter merges into spring, pendulums swing, machines rumble and hearts beat—all in rhythm.

Things are said to be rhythmical when they recur at regular intervals or when their motion can be measured. Music is rhythmical when there is a *regular recurrence* of pulse or accent in a given set of sounds. Most frequently the accent will occur every

two pulses: $/\,/\,/\,/\,/\,/\,/$

or every three: $/\,/\,/\,/\,/\,/\,/\,/$

or every four: $/\,/\,/\,/\,/\,/\,/$

Among other things, rhythm in music makes it possible to distinguish rock from ragtime or a waltz from a square dance.

Overlaid on these regular, recurring accents that make up the basic pulse in music may be heard a *series of long and short sounds* as well as measured silences arranged in various combinations. These are also referred to as *rhythm* or *rhythm patterns*. A succession of sounds of the same duration (length) will produce an *even* rhythm that may be likened to walking:

_____ _____ _____ _____

or at a faster tempo, to running:

—— —— —— —— —— ——

A long sound followed by a short sound produces an *uneven* rhythm pattern that sounds very much like skipping or galloping:

——— —— ——— —— ——— ——

QUESTIONS

1. Rhythm is one of the _ELEMENTS_ of music.
2. Music is said to be rhythmical when there is a regular recurrence of _ACCENT_.
3. Rhythm patterns may be _EVEN_ or _UNEVEN_.

Answers p. 286

BEATS AND BARS

Bar Lines and Measures

Throughout a staff may be found a series of vertical lines. These are called *bar lines* or *measure bars.* They serve to divide any given staff into *measures.* A *double bar* signifies the end of a section or piece of music.

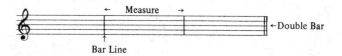

QUESTIONS

4. Vertical lines that divide a staff into measures are called _BAR LINES_ or _MEASURE_ bars.
5. A double bar signifies the _END_ of a piece of music.
6. The space between bar lines is called a _MEASURES_.

Answers p. 286

Each measure in any given piece of music may be expected to contain a specified number of *beats* as determined by the upper figure of the *meter* or *time signature* (see "Meter or Time Signatures," p. 14.)

Beats

The word *beat* has been used here in the context that each measure of a musical piece contains a certain number of beats. What is meant by a *beat*? The *Random House College Dictionary* defines a beat as the "audible, visual or mental marking of the metrical divisions of music." To help clarify the definition, try the following:

1. Clap hands once, saying the word "one" when the clap is sounded and the words "one thousand" while the clap is held.
2. Clap hands again, saying the word "two" when the clap is sounded and the words "one thousand" while the clap is held, as before.
3. Clap hands again, saying the words "three-one thousand" as before.
4. Clap hands again, saying the words "four-one thousand" as before.
5. Clap the entire sequence of four claps, saying the words "one-one thousand, two-one thousand," etc., without hesitation in between.

The four claps sounded in the above exercise represent four beats. Saying the words "one thousand" in between ensures an equal division of time between each beat and a steady flow of the rhythm.

A *metronome* is a mechanical device that keeps time by producing an audible steady beat at any desired pre-set *tempo* (speed). It may be set for a fast or a slow tempo, or for a moderate one in betwen, and will maintain the beat as long as desired.

Meter or Time Signatures (upper figure)

A *meter* or *time signature* is a set of two numbers, one over the other, located to the right of the key signature at the beginning of a piece of music:

The upper figure of any given meter signature indicates the number of beats to be found in each measure of the music as well as provides a clue as to where the *accent* or *strong beat* will occur in the measure. For example, in the meter signature $\frac{2}{4}$ the upper figure 2 indicates that there will be two beats in every measure of that piece and that the accent or strong beat will fall on the first of every two beats. (In the examples below the *accented* beats are shown by longer lines, the *unaccented* or *weak* beats by shorter lines).

In $\frac{3}{4}$ meter the upper figure 3 designates three beats in every measure, with the accent falling on the first of every three beats:

In $\frac{4}{4}$ meter the upper figure 4 designates four beats in every measure, with the accent falling on the first of every four beats:

The upper figure of a meter signature may also be 6, 9, or 12, or other figures such as the less common 5 or 7.

QUESTIONS

7. The set of numbers found at the beginning of a piece of music is called the METER SIGNATURE.

8. The upper figure of the meter signature indicates the number of beats that will be contained in each MEASURE.

9. When the upper figure of the meter signature is 2 there will be ___2___ beats in every measure.

10. There are three beats in every measure of a song containing the meter signature $\frac{3}{4}$ because the UPPER NUMBER IS 3.

11. The upper figure in the meter signature $\frac{4}{4}$ indicates that there
    will be _4 BEATS_ _____ in every
    MEASURE .

12. A meter signature is found at the _COMMENCE_ of a piece
    of music.

Answers p. 286

Conducting Patterns

One way to help maintain the steady beat of any given meter is to practice standard conducting patterns. The upper figure of the meter signature
dictates the appropriate hand directions. Commonly accepted as basic conducting patterns are those shown below:

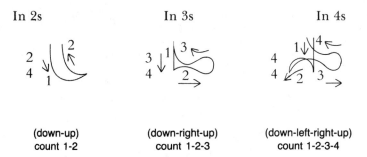

In 2s	In 3s	In 4s
(down-up)	(down-right-up)	(down-left-right-up)
count 1-2	count 1-2-3	count 1-2-3-4

The direction is always *down* on the count of *one* (known as the *downbeat*). This
means that there is a downward motion of the hand on the *first* beat of every
measure, preceded by an upward motion on the preparatory beat:

Preparatory beat   Down beat

Practice conducting patterns to music in different meters.

QUESTIONS

13. In $\frac{2}{4}$ meter the accent or strong beat occurs on the first of
    every _____ (two, four) beats.

14. The accent will fall on the first beat of every three beats in
    _____ meter.

15. When conducting, the first beat of each measure is always in the _____ (downward, upward) direction; the preparatory beat for a downbeat is always in the _____ (downward, upward) direction.

16. In $\frac{4}{4}$ time the downbeat occurs on the _____ beat of each measure.

17. Draw conducting patterns for the following meter signatures, indicating directions by arrows and beats by numbers:

    $\frac{2}{4}$ $\frac{3}{4}$ $\frac{4}{4}$

Answers p. 286

RHYTHM SYMBOLS

Notes are symbols used to represent the long and short sounds that make up rhythm patterns. There are many different kinds of notes in music, representing various time values: ♩, ♩, ♪, ♪, o, etc.

Some notes have solid heads: ♪ Others are open: ♩ Some have stems ♩ Others do not: o

When writing notes with stems on the staff the stem may go up or down depending on the location of the note on the staff. Notes that fall *above* the third line of staff are usually written with the stems going *down*. When the stem goes *down*, it should be placed on the *left* side of the note:

Notes that fall *below* the third line are usually written with the stems going *up*. When the stem goes *up*, it should be placed on the *right* side of the note:

When notes fall *on* the third line, the stem position is left to choice, based on the position of surrounding notes. The up or down position of any note stem is for appearance purposes only. It has *no* effect on the sound of the note.

The Quarter Note ♩

A quarter note is a *closed* (solid head) note with a stem: ♩ To write quarter notes with a minimum of effort, simply make a short horizontal line ▬ then add a stem going either *up* on the *right* side or *down* on the *left* side ┘┌. (When using chalk, select a short piece, make one horizontal stroke the width of the broad side of the chalk, then add stem ⌐ .)

QUESTIONS

18. The symbols used to represent the long and short sounds in music are called _____.

19. A quarter note looks like this: _____.

20. Stems on notes that fall *above* the third line of the staff are written (up, down).

21. Stems going *up* should be placed on the (right, left) side of the notes.

22. Place stems in their appropriate places on the following given noteheads:

Answers p. 286

Meter or Time Signatures (lower figure)

The lower figure of a time signature indicates what kind of note will be used as the unit of beat or, to put it another way, what kind of note will receive one beat.

When the lower figure of the time signature is 4 then a *quarter note* ♩ is the designated unit of beat, meaning that each quarter note will receive one beat:

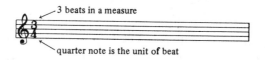

Sometimes a meter signature is written with the note symbol used in place of the lower figure:

$\frac{2}{4}$ would be written 2 $\frac{3}{4}$ would be written 3

In these cases the note symbol means the same as the figure 4—that the quarter note is the unit of beat. Also used occasionally is the symbol 𝐂 representing the $\frac{4}{4}$ meter signature. This is simply an alternate way of writing $\frac{4}{4}$, sometimes called *common time*. Its origin is historical, but it means the same— four beats in each measure, with the quarter note as the unit of beat.

QUESTIONS

23. A quarter note is the unit of beat when the lower figure of the time signature is _____.

24. The unit of beat in $\frac{2}{4}$ meter is the _____.

25. The symbol $\frac{2}{\raisebox{-2pt}{\textbf{J}}}$ means the same as the numbers _____.

26. This symbol $\frac{3}{\raisebox{-2pt}{\textbf{J}}}$ means that there are _____ beats in a measure and the unit of beat is the _____ note.

27. This symbol: _____ means the same as these numbers: $\frac{4}{4}$.

Answers p. 286

Practice Rhythm Patterns for Quarter Note   Chant the following quarter note patterns using the rhythm syllable "ta" (*tah*)—one syllable to each beat. Accent the first beat of each measure as indicated by the accent mark >. Establish desired tempo at the outset:

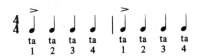

Chant two measures of quarter notes in a different meter, using the same syllable "ta" and accenting the first beat of each measure as before:

A NOTE ABOUT PRACTICE MELODIES: All the practice melodies contained in this chapter and in Chapter 3 are intended to provide application in a melodic setting for the specific rhythm under study. These melodies may be sung with syllables or numbers, played on the recorder, piano or other keyboard instrument, or, if preferred, simply chanted for further rhythm practice, depending on choice of learning sequence. It is suggested, however, that if they are to be sung with syllables or numbers, Chapter 4 be introduced prior to Chapters 2 and 3.

Practice Melodies for Quarter Note

See also Practice Melody no. 2, p. 147.

The song "Old Hundred" is composed entirely of quarter notes. Although $\frac{4}{4}$ meter is indicated, note that there is only one quarter note (thus, one beat) before the first bar line, and three quarter notes (three beats) in the final measure. Any piece of music that begins with an "incomplete" measure will most frequently show the remainder of the required beats (according to the meter signature) in the final measure. (See also "Tallis Canon," p. 199.)

Note also the *fermata*, or hold sign ⌢ over certain notes. This means that the note over which it appears may be held longer than its usual prescribed time, depending upon the wishes of the performer or conductor. Although fermatas interrupt the rhythmic flow, they do add to expressiveness.

OLD HUNDRED

Words by WILLIAM KETHE, 1561
Music by LOUIS BOURGEOIS, 1551

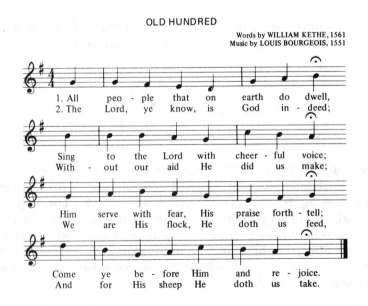

MORE RHYTHM SYMBOLS

The Quarter Rest ♩

Silence is equally as important as sound in music. Notes symbolize sound. *Rests* symbolize silence. For each note there is a corresponding rest that receives the same number of beats of silence — for example, when a quarter note (♩) receives one beat of sound, a *quarter rest* (♩) receives one beat of silence.

quarter *note* — 1 beat of *sound*   quarter *rest* — 1 beat of silence

Beats of silence must be reckoned in when counting the number of beats in a measure, such as:

$$\frac{3}{4} \quad ♩ \; ♩ \; ♩ \; | \; ♩ \; ♩ \; ♩ \quad etc.$$
$$1\;2\;3\;\;|\;1\;2\;3$$

QUESTIONS

28. A rest is a symbol meaning _____.
29. There is a corresponding rest for each _____.
30. When a quarter note gets one beat of sound, a quarter rest gets one beat of _____.
31. In $\frac{3}{4}$ time each ♩ would receive _____ beat(s) of silence.
32. In the following rhythm patterns note the time signature, then insert measure bars in their appropriate places:

A. $\frac{3}{4}$ ♩ ♩ ♩ ♩ ♩ ♩ ♩ ♩ ♩ ♩ ♩ ♩ ♩ ♩ ♩ ♩ ♩ ‖

B. $\frac{2}{4}$ ♩ ♩ ♩ ♩ ♩ ♩ ♩ ♩ ♩ ♩ ♩ ♩ ‖

C. $\frac{4}{4}$ ♩ ♩ ♩ ♩ ♩ ♩ ♩ ♩ ♩ ♩ ♩ ♩ ♩ ♩ ♩ ♩ ‖

Answers pp. 286–289

When executing rhythm patterns containing rests, saying the word "rest" aloud as each one occurs will help to allow the proper time value as well as maintain the flow of the rhythm.

Chant the following, saying "rest" aloud as shown. Establish desired tempo at the outset.

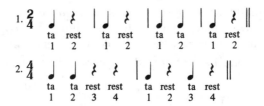

Practice Rhythm Patterns for Quarter Note and Quarter Rest Chant the following rhythm patterns two times each. The first time through say "rest" aloud when one occurs; the second timde through observe one beat of *silence* while thinking the word "rest" as each occurs. Establish a desired tempo before beginning, and keep the beat steady.

Practice Melodies for Quarter Note and Quarter Rest (See **NOTE p. 19**)

4.

Note the quarter rests in the verse of "Sweet Betsy from Pike" shown below.

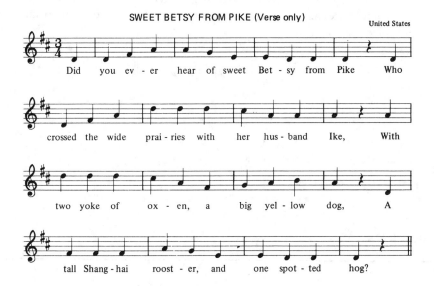

SWEET BETSY FROM PIKE (Verse only)

United States

Did you ev - er hear of sweet Bet - sy from Pike Who

crossed the wide prai - ries with her hus - band Ike, With

two yoke of ox - en, a big yel - low dog, A

tall Shang - hai roost - er, and one spot - ted hog?

The Half Note ♩

The *half note* is an open note head with a stem. It is equal to two quarter notes in time value: ♩ = ♩♩ thus it must be held twice as long as a quarter note. When a quarter note is the unit of beat, a half note gets two beats.

When singing a half note it should be noted that the two beats must be two *full* beats and not merely a portion. To ensure that the second beat be of the same duration as the first, it is suggested that for practice at the outset the first beat be *accented* or *stressed* and the second beat *pulsated*. To *pulsate* means to give a full beat of extra push with the voice on the "ah" sound.

♩   ♩

ta - ah ta - ah
1 - 2   1 - 2

Once the feeling for the sound of the half note has been established, it may be sung in the normal manner (holding steady for the required two beats) with the audible pulsating eliminated.

QUESTIONS

33. A half note is equal to _____ quarter notes.

34. In $\frac{4}{4}$ time a half note gets _____ beats.

35. _____ half note(s) would be required to fill a measure of $\frac{2}{4}$ time.

36. In the following rhythm patterns note the time signature for each pattern, then insert the measure bar in the appropriate place:

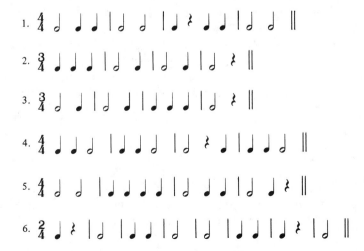

Answers p. 287

Practice Rhythm Patterns for Half Note   Chant the following rhythm patterns two times each. The first time through pulsate the second beat of each half note audibly; the second time through hold each half note for the required two beats while simply "feeling" the pulsation of the second beat. Establish desired tempo at the outset and maintain a steady beat.

Practice Melodies for Half Note (See **NOTE** p. 19)

See also Practice Melodies on the following pages:

  p. 133 (no. 4)
  p. 135 (no. 3)
  p. 145 (nos. 1, 2, and 4)
  p. 150 (nos. 1, 2, and 3)
  p. 155 (nos. 1 and 2)
  p. 158 (nos. 1 and 2)
Note the half notes in the song "Good Night" that follows.

GOOD NIGHT

Good night to you all, and sweet be thy sleep; May an - gels a -

round you their si - lent watch keep, Good night, good night, good night, good night.

The Half Rest ▬

A *half rest* gets the same amount of silence as a half note gets sound.
When a half note gets two beats of sound, a half rest gets two beats of silence:

<table>
<tr><td>▬
half rest
two beats of silence</td><td>♩
half note
two beats of sound</td></tr>
</table>

A half rest is written on the third line of the staff:

QUESTIONS

37. In $\frac{3}{4}$ time a half rest gets _____ 2 _____ beats of silence.
38. The symbol for a half rest is _____ and is always written on the _middle_ line of the staff.
39. The corresponding note for a half rest is a _½ note_ note.
40. In the following rhythm patterns insert the measure bar in the appropriate place according to the meter signature shown:

Answers p. 287

In sounding the half rest during practice say "re-est" to ensure two full beats of silence being observed:

ta - ah   re - est   ta - ah   re - est

ta rest ta rest ta-ah re-est

Practice Rhythm Patterns for Half Rest   Chant the following. Establish tempo and steady beat at the outset.

Practice Melodies for Half Rest (See NOTE p. 19)

See also "Whistle Daughter," p. 137.

The Slur

"Go Tell Aunt Rhody" contains all the rhythms presented so far. It also contains a *slur*, which is a curved line connecting two or more notes of different pitches, signifying that they are to be played or sung smoothly (*legato*) without a break. Note the slur over the syllable "Rho" in the fourth measure. A slur is commonly used when a word or portion of a word extends over several tones of different pitches. Slurs do not affect the length of time notes are to be held.

GO TELL AUNT RHODY

QUESTIONS

41. A slur is a curved line connecting tones of _____ (same, different) pitches

42. A slur indicates that tones are to be sung or played _____.

43. A slur _____ (affects, does not affect) the time values of the notes.

Answers p. 287

The Dotted Half Note 𝅗𝅥.

A *dotted half note* is simply a half note with a dot added: 𝅗𝅥. A dotted half note is equal to three quarter notes: 𝅗𝅥. = ♩♩♩ Thus when the lower figure of a given meter signature is 4, the dotted half note will receive three beats.

QUESTIONS

44. When a quarter note is the unit of beat, a dotted half note receives _____ beats.
45. It takes _____ quarter notes to equal one dotted half note.
46. In ⁴⁄₄ time a dotted half note will receive _____ beats.
47. A dotted half note looks like this: _____.
48. In the following rhythm patterns insert measure bars in the appropriate places according to the meter signature given:

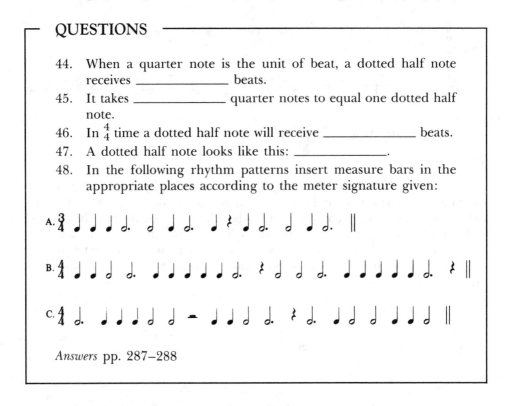

Answers pp. 287–288

When sounding a dotted half note, accent the first beat and pulsate the second and third beats for initial practice (see *Half Note,* p. 23).

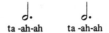

Practice Rhythm Patterns for Dotted Half Note   Chant the following. Establish tempo and steady beat at the outset.

Practice Melodies for Dotted Half Note See NOTE p. 19

See also Practice Melodies on the following pages:

p. 145 (no. 2)
p. 146 ("Lullaby" and "Au Clair de la Lune")
p. 149 (no. 3)
p. 153 (no. 1)
p. 155 (no. 3)
p. 158 (no. 3)

Note the slurs and the full line of dotted half notes in the song below.

LOVELY EVENING

Traditional Round

Oh, how love - ly is the eve - ning, is the eve - ning,

When the bells are sweet - ly ring - ing, sweet - ly ring - ing,

Ding, dong, ding, dong, ding, dong.

Note the slur over the word "no."

RIDDLE SONG

Traditional

2. How can there be a cherry that has no stone?
How can there be a chicken that has no bone?
How can there be a story that has no end?
How can there be a baby that's no crying?

3. A cherry when it's blooming, it has no stone.
A chicken when it's pippin' it has no bone.
The story that I love you, it has no end.
A baby when it's sleeping, it's no crying.

See also pp. 146, 151, 153, and 156 for more songs containing the dotted half note.

The Tie

In the song "Du, Du" below note the curved line extending between the dotted half notes in several measures. When a curved line connects notes of the same pitch it is called a *tie*. A tie may occur within a measure or extend across measure bars:

tie   tie

When singing or playing tied notes, sound the first tone and hold it for the duration of all the notes connected by the tie.

♩♩ = 2 beats

In meter 4/4:

♩♩♩ or ♩♩ = 3 beats

𝅝.♩ or ♩♩ = 4 beats

𝅝.𝅝. = 6 beats

A tie differs from a slur (see p. 27) in that it connects notes of the *same* pitch whereas a slur connects notes of *different* pitches. (See also Practice Melody no. 4, p. 135 and "Morning Has Broken" p. 153.)

Note: The song "Du Du" (as well as many other songs in this book) shows single letter names written above each measure. These letters represent chords that may be used to provide harmonic accompaniment to the melody when desired. (See Chapter 9.)

DU, DU LIEGST MIR IM HERZEN

German

Du, du liegst mir in Herz - en, Du, du
You, you live in my heart dear, You, you

liegst mir im Sinn. Du, du machst mir viel Schmerz - en.
live in my mind. You, you, make me feel sor - row.

Weisst nicht, wie gut ich dir bin?_____ Ja, ja,
Do you not know I love you?_____

ja, ja, Weisst nicht, wie gut ich dir bin?_____
Do you not know I love you?_____

QUESTIONS

49. A curved line connecting two notes of the same pitch is called
    a _____.

50. In 4/4 time this combination of notes ♩♩ would be held for
    _____ beats altogether.

51. A tie _____ (affects, does not affect) the time value of the note.
52. A _____ connects notes of the same pitch; a _____ connects notes of _____ pitches.

Answers p. 288

The Whole Note o

The *whole note* is an open note with no stem. A whole note is equal to four quarter notes o = ♩♩♩♩. When a quarter note is the unit of beat, a whole note receives four beats.

$$o = ♩♩♩♩$$
$$4 \quad 1 \ 1 \ 1 \ 1$$

QUESTIONS

53. When a quarter note is the unit of beat, a whole note receives _____ beats.
54. A whole note has no _____.
55. A whole note receives four beats in _____ time.
56. A whole note is equal to four _____ notes or two _____ notes.

Answers p. 288

When sounding a whole note, accent the first beat and pulsate the second, third and fourth beats during initial practice (see *Half Note*, p. 23):

o   o
ta-ah-ah-ah   ta-ah-ah-ah

Practice Rhythm Patterns for Whole Note   Chant the following. Establish tempo and steady beat at the outset.

Practice Melodies for Whole Note (see NOTE p. 19)

See also Practice Melodies on the following pages:

p. 134 (no. 8)
p. 135 (no. 1)
p. 137 (no. 1)
p. 145 (no. 3)
p. 153 (no. 3)

Note the ties and whole notes in the song that follows.

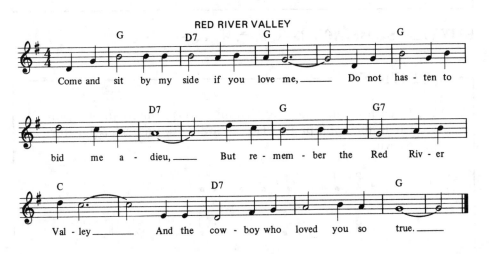

See also "Good King Wenceslas," p. 151.

Whole Rest ▬

A *whole rest* ▬ is used to indicate a complete measure of silence; therefore, the number of beats a whole rest receives may vary according to the upper figure of the meter signature. For example:

In $\frac{3}{4}$ time a whole rest receives three beats (upper figure is 3)
In $\frac{4}{4}$ time a whole rest receives four beats (upper figure is 4)

On the staff the whole rest is written suspended from the fourth line:

QUESTIONS

57. A complete measure of _____ is designated by a whole rest.
58. When written on the staff the whole rest hangs from the _____ line.
59. In $\frac{3}{4}$ time a whole rest receives _____ beats.
60. A whole rest always receives four beats. (True, False)
61. The number of beats a whole rest receives is dependent upon the _____ _____ _____ _____ _____ _____.

Answers p. 288

RHYTHM SUMMARY (♩, 𝄾, 𝅗𝅥, ▬, 𝅘𝅥𝅭, 𝅝, ▬)

QUESTIONS

62. In each of the following rhythm patterns, insert the measure bar in the appropriate place according to the meter signature shown.

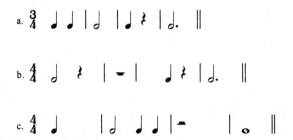

63. According to the meter signatures in the rhythm patterns below, some of the measures shown are rhythmically incomplete. Complete the measures where necessary by adding an appropriate rest or note (*one* only).

Answers p. 288

Chapter Three

More About Rhythm

THE EIGHTH NOTE ♪

An *eighth note* is a solid note head with a stem and a flag: ♪ The stem may be written up: ♪ or down: ♪ Sometimes a *beam* (or bar) is used instead of a flag: ♫ This has no effect on the time value of the note.

It takes two eighth notes to equal one quarter note: ♪ ♪ = ♩ thus eighth notes move twice as fast as quarter notes. When a quarter note receives one beat, an eighth note will receive one half beat.

$$\quad ♩ \;=\; ♪\,♪ $$
$$\quad\; 1 \qquad ½ \; ½$$

An eighth rest has the same time value as an eighth note.

$$\qquad ♪ \qquad\qquad ꜖$$

eighth note eighth rest

QUESTIONS

1. Eighth notes move _____ (slower, faster) than quarter notes.

2. It takes _____ eighth notes to equal one quarter note.

3. When the lower figure of the time signature is 4 each eighth note will receive _____ beat(s).

4. In $\frac{3}{4}$ time two eighth notes equal _____ beat(s).

Answers p. 289

Devices for Practice on Eighth Notes

Several devices may be used as aids for initial practice in sounding eighth notes correctly. A few are suggested below.

Word Patterns   These may be the names of people, food, cars, cities or other categories as long as they are two-syllable words (Kathy, apple, Chrysler, etc.). When practicing in combination with other notes, the quarter note or long sounding word must be a one-syllable word:

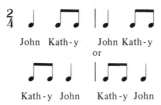

Thus, a rhythm pattern such as this:

might be translated into:

$$\begin{array}{c}\end{array}$$

John	John	Kath-y	John	Kath-y	Kath-y	John	John

or if cars or cities are preferred, into:

Ford	Ford	Chry- sler Ford *etc.*	
Butte	Butte	Dal - las Butte *etc.*	

Long and Short Lines   Long and short horizontal lines, accompanied by the chanting of the words "long" and "short," are sometimes useful as an aid in sounding eighth notes properly:

———————   ———————   ——— ———   ———————
long   long   short   short   long

Rhythm Syllables   Some music systems use one rhythm syllable for quarter notes ("ta") and a different rhythm syllable for eighth notes ("ti"):

ta   ti ti ta   ta

In the interest of expediency, the "ta" (*tah*) and "ti" (*tee*) sounds will be used herein.

Eighth notes commonly appear in pairs. The most common error made in executing two notes within one beat is failure to allot an equal amount of time to each note, resulting in two *unequal* rather than *equal* sounds. The following device may prove helpful in assuring even division of the time value:

1. Rest the elbow on a flat surface with hand in the air.
2. Drop hand down to the surface and bring it back up again, keeping the elbow in contact with the surface.
3. Chant one eighth note on the *down* swing and one on the *up* swing:

♪ ♪

ti   ti

Down up

Since the distance down is exactly the same as it is up, such a movement ensures even distribution of the time. One total movement (down-up) is also equal to the duration of one quarter note:

♩   =   ♫

ta   ti   ti

(down-up)   (down-up)

Practice Rhythm Patterns for Eighth Notes and Eighth Rests   Chant the following rhythm patterns, using the suggetsed elbow swing to help give proper time value to each of the notes and to maintain a steady beat. Establish a slow tempo at the outset. In initial stages of practice try using the sound "oom" on the eighth rests (ɣ) simply as a device to aid the flow of the rhythm. When the rhythm is mastered, the sound should be replaced by silence.

1. $\frac{2}{4}$ ♪ ♪ ♪ ♪ | ♪ ♪ ♪ ♪
   ti ti ti ti   ti ti ti ti

2. $\frac{4}{4}$ ♩ ♪♪♩ ♪♪♩ | ♩ ♪♪♩ ɣ ‖
   ta ti ti ta ti ti

3. $\frac{3}{4}$ ♩ ♩ ♫ | ♩ ♩ ♩ | ♩ ♫ ♫ | ♩ ɣ ‖

4. $\frac{2}{4}$ ♩ ♫ | ♩ ♫ | ♩ ♩ | ♩ ɣ ‖

5. $\frac{4}{4}$ ♩ ♩ ɣ ♪♩ | ♩ ♫ ɣ ♪♩ ‖
   ta   ta oom ti tah

oom ti ta

Practice Melodies for Eighth Notes (See NOTE p. 19)

In "Hush, Little Baby" below, note how the ties in the first and second measures are used to accommodate the one-syllable words in the second verse.

HUSH, LITTLE BABY

American Folk Song

1. Hush,   lit - tle   ba - by,   don't   say   a   word,
2. If   that __   dia - mond   ring   turns __ brass,

Pa - pa's gon - na buy you a mock - ing - bird.
Pa - pa's gon - na buy you a look - ing glass.

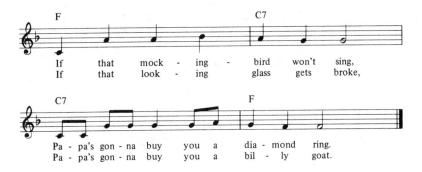

OH, SINNER MAN

Spiritual

See also pp. 136, 138, 146, 147, and 152 for additional songs containing eighth notes.

Dotted Notes and Rests

When a dot appears beside a note it means that the time value of the note is increased by half its original value. For example:

If a ♩ = 2 beats, a ♩. = 3 beats

$$2 + 1 = 3$$

If a 𝅝 = 4 beats, a 𝅝. = 6 beats

$$4 + 2 = 6$$

If a ♩ = 1 beat, a ♩. = 1½ beats

$$1 + \tfrac{1}{2} = 1\tfrac{1}{2}$$

QUESTIONS

5. A dot receives _____ the value of the note which it follows.
6. A dot beside a half note is worth _____ beat(s) in $\frac{3}{4}$ time.
7. A dotted quarter note receives _____ beats in $\frac{2}{4}$ time.
8. If a note receives four beats, a dot beside that note will be worth _____ beats.

Answers p. 289

Rests may also be dotted. When a dot appears beside a rest, the time value of the rest is increased by half its original value in the same manner as notes. For example:

If a ▬ = 2 beats, a ▬. = 3 beats

If a 𝄽 = 1 beat, a 𝄽. = 1½ beats

QUESTIONS

9. In $\frac{4}{4}$ time a dotted half rest receives _____ beats of silence.
10. A dot beside a quarter rest is worth _____ beat(s) in $\frac{3}{4}$ time.
11. When a dot appears beside a rest, the time value of the rest is _____ (increased, decreased) by _____ its original value.

Answers p. 289

The Dotted Quarter and Eighth Note ♩. ♪

The dotted quarter and eighth note rhythm pattern occurs frequently in many songs, some of which are very familiar:

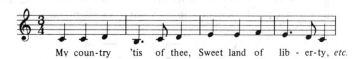

My coun-try   'tis of thee, Sweet land of   lib - er-ty, *etc.*

O   beau - ti - ful   for   spa - cious skies,   For *etc.*

As compared with the pattern of eighth notes that was described as *even,* the dotted quarter and eighth note rhythm is *uneven* because the first tone is longer than the second tone. The uneven rhythm of the ♩. ♪ pattern is more easily understood and executed when broken down into its components—for example, first a quarter note and two eighth notes:

♩   ♪♪♩   ♪♪
ta   ti ti ta   ti ti

Tying the quarter note to the first eighth note in each group of two will indicate that the time value originally given to the first eighth note will now be added to the quarter note in the form of another half beat. (For initial practice purposes this will be pulsated when sung or chanted.)

♩_♪ ♪ ♩_♪ ♪
ta - i ti ta - i ti
(tah - ee)   (tah - ee)

When a dot replaces the eighth note, the pattern sounds the same as in the example above since the dot is of the same value—one half beat:

♩. ♪♩. ♪
ta-i ti ta-i ti

QUESTIONS

12. The dotted quarter and eighth note rhythm is described as _____(even, uneven); the rhythm of two eighth notes as _____ (even, uneven).

13. The time value of the dot in a dotted quarter note is the same as that of an _____ note.

14. In $\frac{4}{4}$ time the dotted quarter note receives _____ beat(s) and the eighth note _____ beat(s).

15. The dotted quarter and eighth note together receive _____ beats.

16. Insert measure bars in appropriate places according to the time signature shown in the following rhythm patterns:

a. $\frac{4}{4}$

b. $\frac{3}{4}$ ♩. ♪♩ ♩ ♫♩ ♩.♪♩ ♫♩ ♩ 𝄽

c. $\frac{4}{4}$ ♩ ♫♩♩. ♪♫♫♩.♪

1 2 + 3

d. $\frac{3}{4}$ ♩ ♩ ♩ | ♫♩ ♩ ♩ | ♩.♪♫ ♩ 𝄽

1 2 3 | 4 + 2 3 | 1 2 + 3 + 1 2 ‖

Answers p. 289

Practice Rhythm Patterns for Dotted Quarter and Eighth Note   Chant the following rhythm patterns. Establish desired tempo at the outset.

- on paper, write out each line
- Do all the conting....

1. $\frac{4}{4}$ ♩. ♪♩. ♪♩ | ♩ ♩ ♩ 𝄽 ‖
   1½ 1 1½ 1 1 1 1

   8 3 + 𝄽

2. $\frac{4}{4}$ ♩ ♫♩. ♪♩ | ♩ ♫♩ ♩ ‖
   1 + +

3. $\frac{3}{4}$ ♩. ♪♩ | ♩. ♪♩ | ♩ ♩ ♩ | ♩. ‖

4. $\frac{2}{4}$ ♩ ♩ | ♩. ♪♩ | ♩ ♩ | ♩ 𝄽 ‖

5. $\frac{4}{4}$ ♩ ♩ ♩. ♪ | ♩. ♪♩ ♩ ‖

6. $\frac{4}{4}$ ♩ ♫♩. ♪♩ | ♩ ♫♩ ♩ ‖

7. $\frac{3}{4}$ ♩. ♪♩ | ♩ ♪♪♩ | ♩. ♪♩ | ♩ 𝄽 ‖

8. $\frac{3}{4}$ ♩ ♩ ♩ | ♩. ♪♩ | ♩ ♩ ♩ | ♩. ‖

9. $\frac{4}{4}$ ♩. ♪♩. ♪♩ | ♩ ♫♩ ♩ 𝄽 ‖

Practice Melodies for Dotted Quarter and Eighth Note (See NOTE p. 19)

The songs that follow contain the dotted quarter and eighth note pattern.

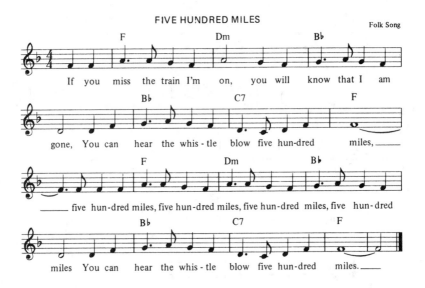

FIVE HUNDRED MILES

Folk Song

If you miss the train I'm on, you will know that I am gone, You can hear the whis-tle blow five hun-dred miles, _____ _____ five hun-dred miles, five hun-dred miles, five hun-dred miles, five hun-dred miles You can hear the whis-tle blow five hun-dred miles. _____

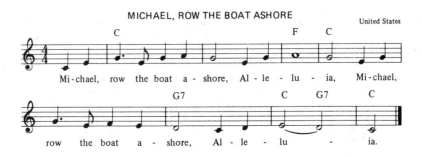

MICHAEL, ROW THE BOAT ASHORE

United States

Mi-chael, row the boat a - shore, Al - le - lu - ia, Mi-chael, row the boat a - shore, Al - le - lu - ia.

See also pp. 147, 148, 151, 152, 155, and 158–59 for additional songs containing dotted quarter and eighth note pattern.

In addition to the ♩⋅ ♪ rhythm, the song "Alouette" below contains several commonly used musical symbols:

1. The *repeat signs* ‖: :‖ indicate a portion of music to be repeated. In this case the music is repeated with words of preceding verses. For example, after singing "et le bec" in verse 3, sing "et le nez" and "et la tete" to the same notes. Follow the same procedure after each verse for verses 4, 5 and 6.
2. *D. C. al Fine* means to go back to the beginning; upon completion of the last verse, end the song at the sign *Fine*.

Note fermata ⌒ over "Oh" in "Alouette" below.

ALOUETTE

French Folk Song

Al - ou-et - te   gen-til al-ou-et - te   Al - ou-et - te

Fine

Je te plum-er-ai   Je te plum-er-ai la tete   Je te plum-er - ai la tete

⌒ *D.C. al Fine*

1. Et la tete   et la tete   Al-ou-ette   Al-ou - ette   Oh _____

2. Je te plumerai le nez 3. Je te plumerai le bec 4. Je te plumerai le cou 5. Je te plumerai le dos 6. Je te plumerai les pattes

Sixteenth Notes ♬

A sixteenth note is a solid note head with a stem and two flags: ♬ ♬ Sixteenth notes may also be written with a double beam: ♬ It takes four sixteenth notes to equal one quarter note; thus if four tones are to be sounded in the time space of one, they must move very quickly. (The more flags on a note, the faster it moves.)

To aid in sounding sixteenth notes during initial practice, the same elbow swing that was used to equalize the distribution of time between two eighth notes may again be used; however, for sixteenth notes there will be *two* tones sounded on the *down* swing and *two* tones on the *up* swing. That means *four* sounds altogether in one complete down-up movement. To illustrate, say these words aloud:

elevator operator

Each of these words has four syllables. Using the elbow swing while speaking the words, say two syllables on the downswing and two on the upswing:

	el-e va-tor	op-er a-tor
Swing:	down up	down up

The musical symbol representing these four sounds is four sixteenth notes.

el - e - va - tor op - er - a - tor

A sixteenth rest ♫ get the same amount of time as a sixteenth note.

QUESTIONS

17. A sixteenth note has _____ flags.
18. Two eighth notes are equal to _____ sixteenth notes.
19. _____ sixteenth notes equal one quarter note.
20. In $\frac{2}{4}$ time four sixteenth notes equal _____ beat(s).
21. It would take _____ sixteenth rests (♫) to equal one quarter rest (𝄽).

Answers p. 289

When sounding sixteenth notes, the rhythm syllables "ti ri ti ri" are sometimes used:

ti   ri   ti   ri

Practice Rhythms for Four Sixteenth Notes   Chant the following rhythm patterns using "ta" on the quarter notes, "ti" on the eighth notes and "ti ri ti ri" on the sixteenth notes, if desired. Using the elbow swing will help to maintain even distribution of time value.

Practice Melodies for Four Sixteenth Notes (See NOTE p. 19)

"Old Brass Wagon" contains the four sixteenth note pattern several times throughout the song.

OLD BRASS WAGON

1. Cir - cle to the left, Old Brass Wag - on,

Cir - cle to the left, Old Brass Wag - on,

Cir - cle to the left, Old Brass Wag - on,

You're   the   one,   my   dar - ling.

The 🎵 and 🎵 Patterns

Eighth notes and sixteenth notes are frequently combined in various patterns such as:

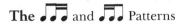

They may be written beamed: ♪♪♪ or with flags: ♪ ♪ ♪

An eighth note combined with two sixteenth notes equals the time value of one quarter note or two eighth notes:

When sounding this pattern, the rhythm syllables "ti" and "ti ri" may be used in combination:

ti   ti - ri   ti - ri   ti

If the elbow swing is used as an aid, the pattern will be *one* sound ("ti") on the downswing and *two* sounds ("ti-ri") on the upswing when written: ♪♪♪ When written: ♪♪♪ the pattern is reversed—two sounds on the downswing, one sound on the up:

ti   ti - ri   ti - ri   ti
down   up   down   up

QUESTIONS

22. The ♪♪♪ pattern is equal in time value to one _____ note.

23. Two _____ notes have the same time value as the ♪♪♪ pattern.

24. Insert measure bars in appropriate places according to the time signature shown in the following rhythm patterns:

Answers p. 289

Practice Rhythm Patterns for  **and** Chant the following rhythm patterns using rhythm syllables "ta", "ti", "ti ri" and "oom" (ﻻ) if desired. Establish desired tempo and steady beat at the outset. Use elbow swing for initial practice.

Practice Melodies for and **(See NOTE p. 19)**

The "Galway Piper" contains all the variations of the sixteenth note patterns presented thus far.

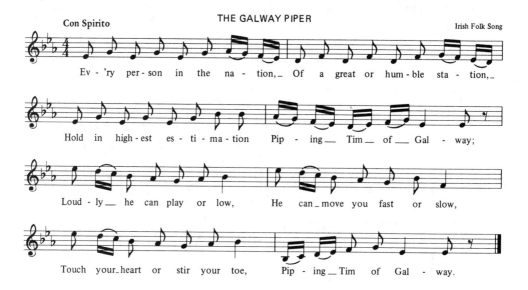

THE GALWAY PIPER

Con Spirito

Irish Folk Song

Ev - 'ry per - son   in   the   na - tion,__ Of   a   great or   hum - ble   sta - tion,__

Hold   in   high - est   es - ti - ma - tion   Pip - ing __ Tim __ of __ Gal - way;

Loud - ly __ he   can play   or   low,   He   can _ move you   fast   or   slow,

Touch   your _ heart   or   stir   your   toe,   Pip - ing __ Tim   of   Gal - way.

The Dotted Eighth and Sixteenth Note Pattern ♪. ♪

Eighth notes, like other notes, may also be dotted. The frequent companion of the dotted eighth note is the sixteenth note or the sixteenth rest. The pattern may be written with a beam: ♪. ♪ or with flags: ♪. ♪

A dotted eighth note followed by a sixteenth note is executed in the same amount of time as two eighth notes or one quarter note. Because the dotted eighth note is longer in time value than the sixteenth note, the rhythm is *uneven* in sound, as in skipping or galloping:

DUM dee   DUM dee   DUM dee

QUESTIONS

25. The sound of the dotted eighth and sixteenth note pattern is _____ (even, uneven).

26. A dotted eighth and sixteenth note together equal the time value of one _____ note or _____ eighth notes.

27. Insert measure bars in the appropriate places according to the time signatures in the following rhythm patterns:

Answers p. 290

Practice Rhythm Patterns for the Dotted Eighth and Sixteenth Note Chant or sound as desired. Establish desired tempo and steady beat at the outset.

Practice Melodies for Dotted Eighth and Sixteenth Note (See NOTE p. 19)

The dotted eighth and sixteenth note pattern is found in many traditional American songs such as those shown below.

OH, SUSANNA

Words and Music by STEPHEN FOSTER

I ___ came from Al - a - ba - ma With my ban - jo on my

knee, I'm ___ going to Loui - si - an - a, My ___

true love for to see? It ___ rained all night the

day I left, The weath - er it was dry; The ___

sun so hot I froze to death; Su - san - na, don't you cry.

Refrain

Oh, Su - san - na, Oh, don't you cry for me, I've__

come from Al - a - ba - ma With my ban - jo on my knee.

SIMPLE GIFTS

Shaker Hymn

'Tis the gift to be sim - ple, 'Tis the gift to be free, 'Tis the

gift to come down where we ought to be, And when we find our - selves__ in the

place just__ right 'Twill__ be in the val - ley of love and de - light.

When true sim - plic - i - ty is gained, To bow and to bend we will

not be a-shamed. To turn,__ to____ turn,__ will__

be our de - light And by turn - ing, turn - ing we come 'round right.

TRAMPIN'

I'm tramp-in', __ tramp-in', __ Tryin' to make heav-en my
home; _____ I'm tramp-in', __ tramp-in', __
Tryin' to make heav-en my home.

VERSE
Solo

1. I've nev-er been to heav-en, but I've been told,
2. Some-times __ I'm __ up, __ some-times I'm down,

Tryin' to make heav-en my home, _____ The streets up there __ are
Tryin' to make heav-en my home, _____ Some-times my soul __ feels

paved with gold. Tryin' to make heav-en my home.
heav'n-ly bound.. Tryin' to make heav-en my home.

BATTLE HYMN OF THE REPUBLIC

HOWE-STEFFE

Mine eyes have seen the glo-ry of the com-ing of the Lord; He is
tram-pling out the vin-tage where the grapes of wrath are stored; He hath
loosed the fate-ful light-ning of His ter-ri-ble swift sword; His truth is march-ing

Chorus:
on. Glo-ry, glo-ry, hal-le-lu-jah! Glo-ry, glo-ry, hal-le-lu-jah!

Glo - ry, glo - ry, hal - le - lu - jah! His truth is march - ing on.

The Triplet

A *triplet* consists of three tones that equal the time value of two of the same kind. It is usually identified by a group of three tones beamed together with a figure 3 over the beam:

It is frequently used to accommodate words such as "merrily" as shown in the song excerpt below without having to change the meter temporarily in order to make them fit:

When I walk mer-ri - ly down the street *etc.*

To sound triplets with rhythm syllables, the words "triple tee" are some-times used:

ta   ta   tri - ple tee ta

Practice Rhythm Patterns for the Triplet   Chant or sound the following rhythm patterns. Establish desired tempo and steady beat at the outset.

Practice Melodies for Triplet (See NOTE p. 19)

In the song "Everybody Loves Saturday Night" note how the word "Saturday" is accommodated by the triplet. ("Everybody Loves Saturday Night" may be sung as a round. Numbers denote voice entrances.)

EVERYBODY LOVES SATURDAY NIGHT

African Folk Song

In "Jesu, Joy of Man's Desiring" the triplet accommodates only one syllable.

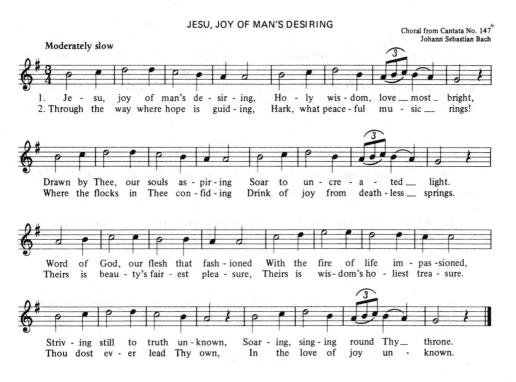

JESU, JOY OF MAN'S DESIRING

Choral from Cantata No. 147
Johann Sebastian Bach

In "Once to Every Man and Nation" the triplet is in the form of quarter notes.

ONCE TO EVERY MAN AND NATION

Welsh Melody (Ton-y-Botel)
Words by James Russell Lowell

•Syncopation

Syncopation is frequently defined as "displaced accent," meaning that the accented or strong beat is displaced from where it would normally occur. In a given measure of $\frac{4}{4}$ time, for example, it is assumed that the primary accent will fall on the first beat, with a secondary accent on the third beat:

Under certain conditions, however, the stress or accent may fall elsewhere than normally expected. Such conditions include:

1. when rests occur on the strong beats, with sound on the weak beats:

2. when certain dynamic symbols direct that stress be placed on the weak beats:

3. when a note of longer duration falls between two notes of shorter duration:

4. or when the presence of a tie produces the same effect:

The result of all these circumstances is syncopation.

QUESTIONS

28. Syncopation may be defined as _____.
29. In $\frac{4}{4}$ time the accents usually occur on the _____ and _____ beats of the measure.
30. Sounding weak beats and resting on strong beats will produce a _____ effect.

Answers p. 290

Practice Rhythms for Syncopation Chant the following rhythm patterns or sound as desired. Establish tempo and steady beat at the outset.

The verse below contains syncopation and is designed to be spoken to the accompaniment of a steady beat. Percussion instruments alone or chording instruments may be used if desired (see Chapter 10, "Chording Instruments," p. 265).

I'm a fast talk-ing wom-an Got a slow talk-ing man and I

Do the best that a wom-an can Lots of love

lots of fight We'll make it all right.

Practice Melodies for Syncopation *(See Note p. 19)*

In the songs that follow, identify the places where syncopation occurs.

BONES

Folk Song from Southern United States

3. Oh, the hip bone connected to the back bone,
   And the back bone connected to the neck bone,
   And the neck bone connected to the head bone,
   Oh, didn't it rain!

WALK TOGETHER, CHILDREN

Spiritual

Oh, walk to-geth-er chil-dren don't you get __ wea - ry Walk to-geth-er chil-dren don't you get wea-ry. Oh, walk to-geth-er chil-dren don't you get __ wea-ry. There's a great camp meet-ing in the prom-ised land.

NO MAN IS AN ISLAND

Contributed by J. FRASER
Canadian (Nova Scotian)

No man is an is-land, No man stands a-lone; Each man's joy is joy to me, Each man's grief is my own; We need one an-oth-er, So I will de-fend Each man as my broth-er, Each man as my friend. I saw the peo-ple gath-er, I heard the mu-sic start, The song that they were sing-ing is ring-ing in my heart.

PALLET ON THE FLOOR

Note: A countermelody for "Pallet on the Floor" can be found on p. 202.

ROCK-A MY SOUL

HE'S GOT THE WHOLE WORLD IN HIS HANDS

Slowly

Spiritual

He's got the whole ___ world ___ in his hands, ___ He's got the whole ___ world ___ in his hands, ___ He's got the whole ___ world ___ in his hands, ___ He's got the whole world in his hands. ___

I'VE GOT A ROBE

Spiritual

I've got a robe you've got a robe All God's chil-dren got a robe When I get to heav-en gon-na put on my robe I'm gon-na walk all o-ver God's heav-en ___ heav-en ___ Ev-'ry-bod-y's talk-in' 'bout heav-en ain't go-in' there heav-en ___ heav-en ___ Gon-na walk all o-ver God's heav-en. ___

2. I've got shoes, you've got shoes etc. (Gonna walk all over God's heaven)
3. I've got wings, you've got wings etc. (Gonna fly all over God's heaven)
4. I've got a voice, you've got a voice etc. (Gonna sing all over God's heaven)
Add other verses as desired.

PEACE LIKE A RIVER

Traditional

I've got peace like a riv-er,

I've got peace like a riv-er,

Meter Signatures (lower figures other than 4)

In all of the foregoing examples of meter signatures, the lower figure has been 4—designating the quarter note as the unit of beat. Upon this was based the time values of all the other notes in a given song. Although not as common as 4, such figures as 2 or 8 may also appear as the lower figure, signifying a different unit of beat. In such cases the time value of all other notes must also change since they are reckoned accordingly based on the unit of beat. For example, when the lower figure is 2 as in $\frac{3}{2}$, $\frac{4}{2}$, or $\frac{2}{2}$ time, the unit of beat is a half note. Thus, if a half note ♩ = 1 beat, then

a whole note 𝅝 = 2 beats
a quarter note ♩ = ½ beat
a dotted half note ♩. = 1½ beats.

Time values for dotted notes are reckoned in the same manner as before, the dot receiving half the value of the note.

Alla Breve Symbol The *alla breve* symbol ₵ (sometimes referred to as *cut time*) designates a halving of the meter from $\frac{4}{4}$ to $\frac{2}{2}$ with the resulting change in the unit of beat from a quarter note to a half note.

QUESTIONS

31. When the lower figure of the meter signature is 2, the unit of beat is a _____ note.

32. The meter signature $\frac{3}{2}$ means _____ beats in a measure with a _____ note as the unit of beat.
33. In $\frac{3}{2}$ meter a half note would receive _____ beat(s).
34. The *alla breve* symbol is _____.
35. In $\frac{4}{2}$ time it would take _____ half notes to fill a measure.

Answers p. 290

Note the alla breve symbol ¢ in the following songs.

THE WATER IS WIDE
(WALY WALY)

English Folk Song

Smooth, flowing

The wa - ter is wide, ___ I can-not get o'er,
And nei - ther have ___ I wings to ___ fly.
Oh, go and get ___ me some lit - tle boat
To car - ry o'er ___ my true love and I. ___

GONNA BUILD A MOUNTAIN

From the musical production "STOP THE
WORLD–I WANT TO GET OFF"
Words and Music by Leslie Bricusse and
Anthony Newley
© Copyright 1961 TRO Essex Music Ltd.,
London, England.
TRO-Ludlow Music Inc. New York controls all
publication rights for the U.S.A. and Canada.
Used by permission.

Gon-na build a moun-tain From a lit - tle hill.
Gon-na build a moun-tain Least I hope I will.

When the lower figure of the meter signature is 8 (as in $\frac{6}{8}$) an eighth note ♪ is the unit of beat. When an eighth note = 1 beat,

a quarter note ♩ = 2 beats
a half note 𝅗𝅥 = 4 beats
a sixteenth note ♬ = ½ beat
a dotted half note 𝅗𝅥. = 6 beats
a dotted quarter note ♩. = 3 beats (♩ + . = 3)

Frequently, when the lower figure is 8, the upper figure is 6, 9 or 12. These are what are sometimes referred to as *compound meters*.

QUESTIONS

36. When the lower figure of the time signature is 8, the unit of beat is an _____ note.
37. In $\frac{9}{8}$ time a quarter note would get _____ beats.
38. In $\frac{6}{8}$ time this measure ♩ ♪ ♩ could be completed by using an_____ note.
39. A single _____ note would completely fill a measure of $\frac{6}{8}$ time.

Answers p. 290

Compound Meters

Thus far the only meters used have been those commonly known as *simple meters*—those in which the upper figure has been 2, 3 or 4. There are other meters in music known as *compound meters* or *compound time*. Whether a piece of music is written in simple or compound time may be determined by dividing the upper figure of the meter signature by three. If three will go into the upper figure *more than once evenly*, the music is written in compound time. If not, the music is written in simple time. Using this formula, 6, 9 and 12 are found to be compound meters.

QUESTIONS

40. Two kinds of meters in music are _____ and compound.

41. $\frac{9}{8}$ is considered a _____ meter; $\frac{4}{4}$ is considered a _____ meter.

42. The _____ (upper, lower) figure of the time signature is what determines whether the meter is simple or compound.

Answers p. 290

Although the lower figure of the time signature is not a factor when determining whether the music is written in simple or compound time, it does provide a clue as to the kind of note groupings one may expect to find in a given piece of music. Compound time has a different kind of a swing than simple time. In compound time the eighth notes often travel in groups of three, and the accents tend to fall on the initial beat of each group of three eighth notes:

$$\frac{6}{8} \quad \overset{>}{1}\ 2\ 3\ \overset{>}{4}\ 5\ 6$$

$$\frac{9}{8} \quad \overset{>}{1}\ 2\ 3\ \overset{>}{4}\ 5\ 6\ \overset{>}{7}\ 8\ 9$$

$$\frac{12}{8} \quad \overset{>}{1}\ 2\ 3\ \overset{>}{4}\ 5\ 6\ \overset{>}{7}\ 8\ 9\ \overset{>}{10}\ 11\ 12$$

Note that the $\frac{6}{8}$ meter falls into *two* main beats or pulses, the $\frac{9}{8}$ into *three* main beats or pulses, and the $\frac{12}{8}$ into *four* main beats or pulses. Since $\frac{9}{8}$ and $\frac{12}{8}$ occur much less frequently in traditional song material, the majority of the examples shown herein will be in $\frac{6}{8}$ meter. What is true for one compound meter holds true for all.

Three eighth notes in compound time sound very much like the triplet in simple time (p. 55). In fact, the word "merrily" used for the triplet is also representative of the sound of three eighth notes in compound time. Note the second line in "Row, Row, Row Your Boat" below:

ROW, ROW, ROW YOUR BOAT

Four-part round

Row,   row,   row   your boat   Gen - tly down   the   stream. ___

Mer - ri - ly, mer - ri - ly,   mer - ri - ly, mer - ri - ly,   Life   is   but   a   dream. —

"Hickory dickory" also works well as a word pattern to use for remembering how to sound the three eighth note pattern in compound time:

Hick - o - ry   dick - o - ry

If rhythm syllables are preferred, "ti" may be used for the eighth notes in compound time as they were in simple time:

$\frac{6}{8}$ ♫♫ ♫♫

ti   ti   ti   ti   ti   ti

In this meter a quarter note receives two beats and an eighth note one beat; thus a sequence of quarters and eighths (♩♪ ♩♪) will produce an *uneven* rhythm. Using the words "Humpty Dumpty" will help sound the quarter and eighth note sequence:

$\frac{6}{8}$ ♩ ♪♩ ♪

Hump - ty dump - ty

The first line of "Humpty Dumpty" contains the three most commonly found rhythm patterns in compound time; thus it might prove helpful for initial practice in learning to sound them correctly:

$\frac{6}{8}$ ♩ ♪♩ ♪ | ♪ ♪ ♪ ♩.

Hump - ty dump - ty   sat   on   a   wall

Compound meter is frequently found in traditional song literature:

A - las   my   love — you   do   me   wrong — to *etc. (Greensleeves)*

$\frac{6}{8}$ ♫♫ ♩ ♪ | ♫♫ ♩

Here   we   go 'round   the   mul - ber - ry   bush *etc.*

as well as in more recent compositions:

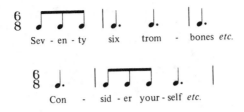

Sev - en - ty   six   trom - bones *etc.*

Con - sid - er your - self *etc.*

QUESTIONS

43. There are _____ main pulses in $\frac{6}{8}$ time.

44. $\frac{12}{8}$ time has _____ main pulses.

45. There are three main pulses in _____ time.

46. When the lower figure of the meter signature is 8, a dotted quarter note receives _____ beats.

47. This rhythm pattern ♩♪♩♪ _____ (will, will not) fill a measure of $\frac{9}{8}$ time.

48. In the rhythm patterns shown below, some of the measures are incomplete. Fill in the appropriate note or rest (one only) where needed in the measure.

a. $\frac{6}{8}$ ♪♪♪♪ ♩ | ♩. ‖

b. $\frac{9}{8}$ ♩. ♪♪♪ | ♩ ♪♪ ♩ ♪♪♪ ‖

Answers p. 290

Practice Rhythm Patterns for Compound Meter Chant the following rhythm patterns. Establish desired tempo and steady beat at the outset.

Do counting for 25th

Practice Melodies for Compound Meter (See NOTE p. 19)

Conducting Patterns for Compound Meters

When there are six beats in a measure and the music moves at a slow tempo, the following conducting pattern in six is used:

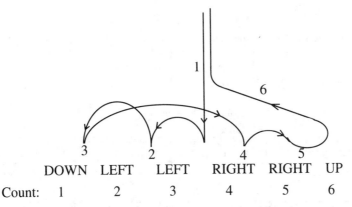

	DOWN	LEFT	LEFT	RIGHT	RIGHT	UP
Count:	1	2	3	4	5	6

When there are six beats in a measure and the music moves at a fast tempo, the conductor beats only the main pulses; the *two*-beat pattern would be used rather than the six-beat pattern, with the beats grouped as follows:

Down   Up

1-2-3   4-5-6

(See "Conducting Patterns," p. 16)

The tempo of "Pop Goes the Weasel" (p. 17) and "Paddy Works on the Railway" (p. 72) dictates that they be conducted with the two-beat pattern, whereas "Silent Night" (p. 223) moves at a much slower tempo, thus the six-beat pattern would be more appropriate. When there are nine beats in a measure and the music moves at a slow tempo the following conducting pattern in nine is used:

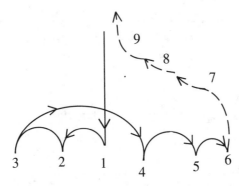

	DOWN	LEFT	LEFT	RIGHT	RIGHT	RIGHT	UP	UP	UP
Count:	1	2	3	4	5	6	7	8	9

When there are nine beats in a measure and the music moves at a fast tempo, the *three*-beat pattern would be used with the beats grouped as follows:

	(1)	(2)	(3)
Arm movement:	Down	right	up
Beat grouping:	1 − 2 − 3	4 − 5 − 6	7 − 8 − 9

(See "Conducting Patterns," p. 16)

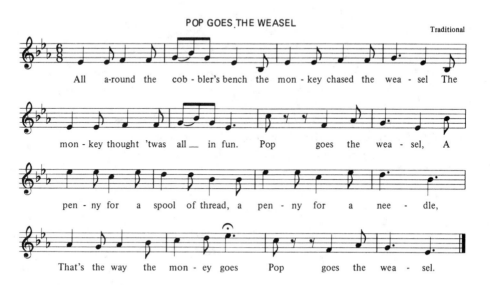

POP GOES THE WEASEL

Traditional

All a-round the cob - bler's bench the mon - key chased the wea - sel The

mon - key thought 'twas all __ in fun. Pop goes the wea - sel, A

pen - ny for a spool of thread, a pen - ny for a nee - dle,

That's the way the mon - ey goes Pop goes the wea - sel.

PADDY WORKS ON THE RAILWAY

Solo Gm   Bb   Irish-American Railroad Song

1. In eight-een hun-dred and for-ty-one I put my cor-du-roy breech-es on, I

Gm   D7   Gm

put my cor-du-roy breech-es on to work up-on the rail-way.

Chorus
REFRAIN
Gm   Bb

Fil - li - mee - oo - ree - oo - ree - ay, Fil - li - mee - oo - ree - oo - ree - ay,

Gm   D7   Gm

Fil - li - mee - oo - ree - oo - ree - ay, to work up-on the rail-way.

2. In eighteen hundred and forty-two
I left the old world for the new,
Oh, spare me the luck that brought me through
To work upon the railway. *(Refrain)*

3. It's "Pat, do this," and "Pat, do that,"
Without a stocking or cravat,
And nothing but an old straw hat,
While working on the railway. *(Refrain)*

Note: A countermelody for the *refrain* of "Paddy Works on the Railway" can be found on p. 202.

"We're All Together Again" is representative of the vigorous kind of song frequently set in compound time, whereas "Greensleeves" is of the more gentle variety. Determine the most appropriate conducting pattern for each.

"Down in the Valley" (p. 216) is in $\frac{9}{8}$ meter. Does the spirit of the song suggest the slow nine-beat conducting pattern or the fast three-beat one?

Which conducting pattern seems most appropriate for the following two songs in $\frac{6}{8}$ meter? (Portions shown may be sung as partner songs—see p. 195.)

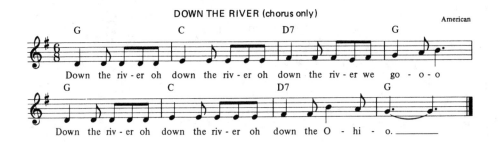

DOWN THE RIVER (chorus only)

American

Down the riv-er oh down the riv-er oh down the riv-er we go - o - o

Down the riv-er oh down the riv-er oh down the O - hi - o.___

VIVE L'AMOUR (chorus only)

Student Song

Vi - ve la vi - ve la vi - ve l'a-mour vi - ve la vi - ve la

vi - ve l'a-mour vi - ve l'a-mour vi - ve l'a-mour ve - ve la com - pa - gnie.___

See other songs in compound meters on pp. 135, 223, and 257.

The traditional "Wassail Song" contains two different meters. Consider whether or not the conducting pattern would change.

HERE WE COME A-WASSAILING

Old English Carol

1. Here   we   come   a - was - sail - ing,   A - mong   the   leaves   so
2. We are   not   dai - ly   beg -   gars   That   beg   from   door   to
3. God bless   the   mas - ter   of   the   house   And   the   mis - tress

green,___   Here   we   come a - wan - d'ring   So   fair___   to   be   seen;
door,   But   we   are neigh-bors' chil - dren Whom you   have   seen   be - fore;
too,   And   all   the   lit - tle   chil - dren That 'round the   ta - ble   go:

Love and joy come to you, And to you your was - sail

too, And God bless you, and send — you a hap - py New

Year, And God send you a hap - py New — Year.

Tempo, Dynamics, and Expression Terms

Arm movements are but one of many concerns of a conductor. Instruments must be cued in at appropriate times, proper tempos established and maintained, and musical works interpreted as each composer intended. The latter requires an in-depth study of the composer's life and musical style as well as careful adherence to the musical "directions" relating to such elements as tempo, dynamics, and expression indicated in the score. Aware of what may happen to a piece of music when these elements are left to the conductor's whim, composers frequently mark their music with very specific tempo, dynamics and expression terms. In fact, some musical works have come to be known by their tempo designation, as "Andante" from *Symphony No. 94* by Haydn and "Largo" from the opera *Xerxes* by Handel. Some of the more commonly used terms are listed below.

TEMPO

HOW FAST OR SLOW

A TEMPO	resume original tempo
ACCELERANDO	gradually growing faster (abbrev. *accel.*)
ALLEGRETTO	rather fast
ALLEGRO	fast
ANDANTE	moderately slow
ANDANTINO	rather slow
LARGO	very slow
LENTO	slow
MODERATO	at a moderate pace
PRESTO	very fast
RITARDANDO	gradually growing slower (abbrev. *rit.* or *ritard.*)

DYNAMICS — INTENSITY
HOW LOUD OR SOFT

		Symbol or abbreviation
CRESCENDO	gradually growing louder	cresc. ⏞
DIMINUENDO	gradually growing softer	dim. ⏟
FORTE	loud	f
FORTISSIMO	very loud	ff
MEZZO FORTE	moderately loud	mf
MEZZO PIANO	moderately soft	mp
PIANISSIMO	very soft	pp
PIANO	soft	p
SFORZANDO	explosively	sf

EXPRESSION

LEGATO	smoothly connected SLUR
MAESTOSO	majestically
SOSTENUTO	sustained ——— TIE
SPIRITO	spiritedly (LIVELY)
STACCATO	disconnectedly
VIVACE	vivaciously

From the foregoing definitions perhaps it may be better understood why the same piece of music performed under several different conductors may vary greatly in interpretation.

Other terms and symbols are defined in the Glossary, p. 301.

ACTIVITIES

The following activities are suggested as aids to better understanding of some of the many facets of rhythm.

1. Clap a rhythm pattern. Have group imitate.
2. Clap melody rhythm of a familiar song. Have group identify the song.
3. Have half the group clap the melody rhythm of a familiar song while the other half taps the steady beat of the meter with the feet, then have total group do both simultaneously.
4. Execute a rhythm canon, with the leader always one measure ahead; for example:

Leader:

Group: *etc.*

Use the same sound (clapping, snapping fingers, vocal sound or other) throughout or vary the sounds in different measures. (Group must be alert to the upcoming pattern while executing the previous one.)

5. Have half the group sound quarter notes while the other half sounds eighth notes simultaneously, using any sounds desired.

6. Repeat as in no. 5 above using three or four groups, with a different kind of note assigned to each group to sound. For variation, add a syncopated rhythm pattern against the others.

7. Divide into two groups and execute some "questions and answers" in rhythm; for example:

Vary rhythms as desired. Substitute different sounds for Q and A.

8. Reinforce the feeling for different meters by executing one movement on the first beat of the meter and a different movement on the remaining beats; for example:

   $\frac{3}{4}$ Pat knees on 1, snap fingers on 2 and 3.

   $\frac{4}{4}$ Tap foot on 1, clap hands on 2, 3 and 4.

   For variation, use percussion instruments—one instrument on the accented beat, another on the unaccented beats.

9. Using drum sticks or suitable substitute, create some rhythm patterns and execute to music in various tempos:

   L = left stick
   R = right stick

Play the following score to "When the Saints Go Marching In" (p. 196).

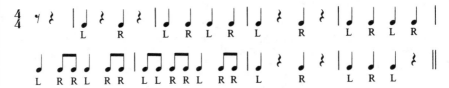

Create some original scores to be played with songs of choice.

10. Below is a simple score for selected instruments to use with "Jingle Bells" (p. 148). (B = bells; Tri = triangle; Tam = tambourine; r = rap; sh = shake; St = sticks; D = drum; WB = wood block; C = cymbals)

Create original scores for selected instruments and play with songs of choice.

11. In the following percussion ensemble select a different rhythm instrument to sound each of the given patterns. Play only on circled beats. Create new patterns by circling different numbers.

AFRICAN PERCUSSION ENSEMBLE

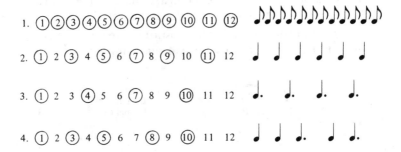

5. ① 2 ③ 4 ⑤⑥ 7 ⑧ 9 ⑩ 11 ⑫

6. ① 2 ③ ④⑤ 6 ⑦⑧⑨ 10 ⑪ ⑫

12. Try "Short March for Percussion" using the instruments suggested or a combination of others.

SHORT MARCH FOR PERCUSSION

FRANK FOX

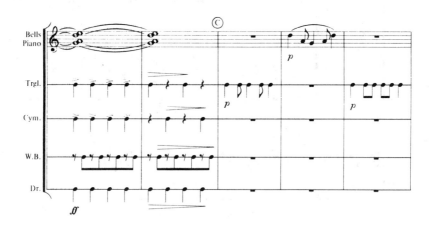

Chapter Four

Singing Major Scale Syllables and Melodies

MAJOR SCALE SYLLABLES

A scale is a series of notes arranged in a specified order. Each tone has a name, sometimes referred to as a *syllable*. The syllable names of the tones of the major scale are DO RE MI FA SOL LA TI DO arranged in that order when the scale *ascends* (read up):

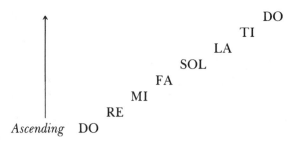

When the major scale *descends,* the order of the syllable names is reversed (read down):

Each syllable represents a different *pitch*. Pitch refers to the highness or lowness of a musical sound.

Try singing the ascending and descending major scale syllables starting on any comfortable pitch.

The method of music reading by syllables is said to have originated with a medieval monk, Guido of Arezzo. In the old Latin hymn "Ut queant laxis," the beginning of each phrase represents a note of the major scale, except for *Ut,* which was later changed to DO; and TI, which was added after LA.

Ut queant laxis
*Re*sonare fibris
*Mi*ra gestorum
*Fa*muli tuorum
*Sol*ve polluti
*La*bii reatum
Sancte Joannes

In this particular hymn the initial tones of each line fell on a successively higher pitch.

Scale Numbers

Sometimes numbers are used in place of syllables to indicate the different tones of the scale, with numbers based on the position of the note in the scale sequence:

```
                                    DO
                              TI  8
                          LA  7
                      SOL  6
                  FA    5
              MI  4
          RE  3
      DO  2
        1
```

Try singing the scale with numbers, ascending first then descending, starting on any comfortable pitch.

Writing Scales on the Staff

(The o symbol used in examples throughout this section denotes pitch only and has no time value.)

A major scale ascending and descending appears as follows when written on the staff—each note placed adjacent to the next on succeeding lines and spaces:

DO may be anywhere on the staff as illustrated in the two examples below:

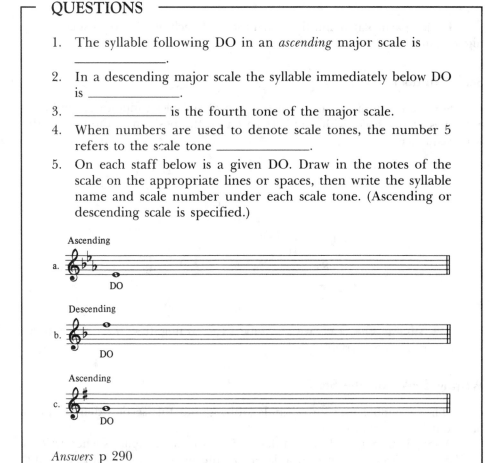

QUESTIONS

1. The syllable following DO in an *ascending* major scale is

    _____.

2. In a descending major scale the syllable immediately below DO
    is _____.

3. _____ is the fourth tone of the major scale.

4. When numbers are used to denote scale tones, the number 5
    refers to the scale tone _____.

5. On each staff below is a given DO. Draw in the notes of the
    scale on the appropriate lines or spaces, then write the syllable
    name and scale number under each scale tone. (Ascending or
    descending scale is specified.)

Ascending

a.

DO

Descending

b.

DO

Ascending

c.

DO

Answers p 290

STEPWISE MELODIES

In One Direction

When major scale tones are organized in various ways a melody results. The melodies shown below all move in *stepwise progression*. A stepwise progression is one in which one scale tone moves to a scale tone immediately adjacent to it:

```
                    FA              DO
            MI                  TI
                      or
      RE                      LA
DO                                  SOL
```

When stepwise melodies are written on the staff, each succeeding note is placed on the line or space immediately adjacent to the preceding note:

DO DO RE RE MI FA SOL SOL

Each stepwise melody shown below is written two ways: (1) off the staff in the direction it moves (up or down) and (2) as the same melody would appear on the staff.

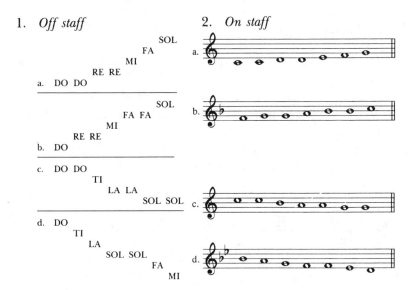

1. *Off staff*   2. *On staff*

Try singing the above melodies at a slow tempo, first from the syllable names shown under (1) then from the staff under (2).

In Two Directions

The following stepwise melodies move in *two* directions—up *and* down. Like the preceding examples, they are written in the direction they move. Try singing each melody at a slow tempo, first from the syllable names under (1), then from the staff under (2).

1. *Off staff*   2. *On staff*

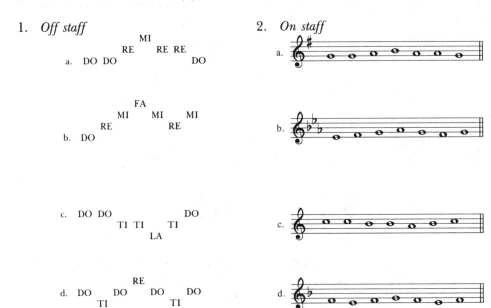

QUESTIONS

6. _____ refers to the highness or lowness of a musical sound.

7. Organizing pitches in various ways can produce a _____.

8. When one scale tone moves to the next scale tone immediately adjacent to it the progression is called _____.

9. In the staves below write the notes in their appropriate places according to the syllables shown (initial DO is given). Sing when completed.

a.   DO   DO   TI   LA   LA   SOL   SOL

b.   DO   RE   RE   MI   FA   FA   SOL

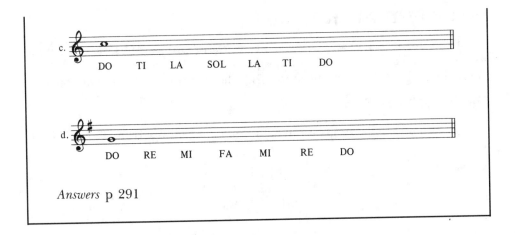

c. DO   TI   LA   SOL   LA   TI   DO

d. DO   RE   MI   FA   MI   RE   DO

Answers p 291

Practice Stepwise Melodies on Staff (two directions)

Sing the following melodies at a slow tempo.

1. DO TI LA SOL LA TI DO DO

2. DO

3. DO

4. DO

Create some original melodies on the order of the foregoing (stepwise in two directions). Add rhythm if desired. (See Chapters 2 and 3.)

MELODIES THAT SKIP

All of the previous melodies have been in *stepwise* progressions. Melodies may also move by *skip*, that is, they may skip over one or more tones in place of simply moving to the adjacent tone. This allows a greater variety of sound.

The DO MI SOL Skip

A common skip progression is the one that moves from DO to MI to SOL.

```
                        SOL
                         5
                MI              MI
                3                3
        DO                              DO
        1                                1
```

When high DO is added, the resulting sound is very much like the opening notes of many songs ranging from "On Top of Old Smokey" to "I Could Have Danced All Night."

```
                        DO
                         8
                SOL             SOL
                 5               5
        MI                              MI
         3                               3
    DO                                        DO
     1                                         1
```

Practice Progressions

Try singing the following progressions as an aid to sounding the DO MI SOL skip:

```
                                                    SOL SOL
                                               FA
            MI MI        MI    MI    MI
        RE          RE  / \ / \ /
A.  DO              DO    DO    DO
```

```
            SOL     SOL     SOL
        FA / \ / \ / \
        MI    MI    MI    MI
                            \
                             DO
```

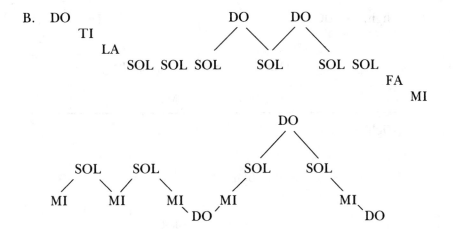

B.   DO
       TI
          LA
             SOL SOL SOL   SOL   SOL SOL
                                              FA
                                                 MI

                                   DO
              SOL   SOL   SOL   SOL
          MI   MI   MI   MI   MI
                               DO   DO

Practice Melodies for DO MI SOL Skip (Off staff)

                                        SOL

                         MI   MI   MI

1. (Low) → DO   DO   DO

2. (High) → DO   DO

                         SOL   SOL   SOL
                                 MI   MI

3. (High) → DO   DO

                                            LA   LA
                         SOL   SOL   SOL

                            SOL   SOL

                         MI   MI
                                            RE
4. (Low) → DO   DO

                         SOL   SOL

                         MI   MI   MI

5. (Low) → DO   DO

6. (High) →   DO   DO

                   SOL   SOL   SOL

                         MI   MI

---

7. (High) →   DO

                   SOL   SOL

                         MI   MI

                             RE

                                  DO

                         SOL   SOL

                      MI

                  RE

8. (Low) →   DO   DO   DO

---

9. (High) →   DO

                   SOL   SOL   SOL

                       FA   FA

                          MI

                       SOL   SOL

                  MI   MI   MI

               RE

10. (Low) →   DO

Writing DO MI SOL Skips on Staff

When melodies containing skips are written on the staff, there will be intervening lines and spaces between the skipping notes:

Skipping   Stepwise

When low DO is on a *space*, MI and SOL above fall on the *spaces* directly above DO:

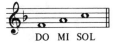

DO MI SOL

When low DO is located on a *line*, MI and SOL above fall on the *lines* directly above DO:

DO MI SOL

QUESTIONS

10. Below are some given DO's. Write in the MI and SOL above each DO:

a.   DO MI SOL   b.   DO MI SOL   c.   DO MI SOL   d.   DO MI SOL

11. In the staves below write the notes in their appropriate places according to the syllables given (initial DO is shown in place).

1.   DO   DO   MI   MI   SOL   SOL   MI   DO

2.   DO   SOL   SOL   DO   MI   RE   RE   DO
         (below)

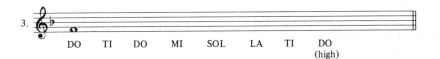

3.   DO   TI   DO   MI   SOL   LA   TI   DO
                                         (high)

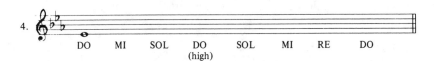

4.   DO   MI   SOL   DO   SOL   MI   RE   DO
                    (high)

Answers p 291

Practice Melodies on Staff for DO MI SOL Skip

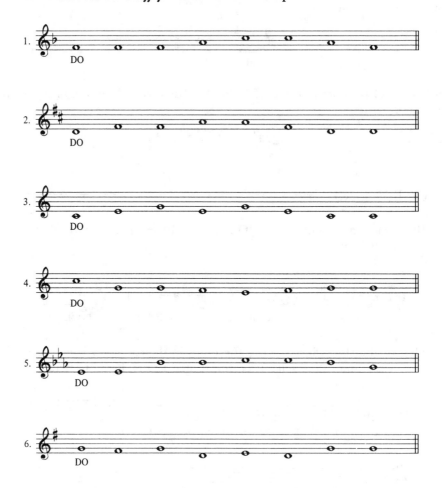

Many traditional songs begin with the DO MI SOL skip. See pp. 23, 44, 153 and 156.

Skips Other Than DO MI SOL

Melodies may also contain skips other than DO MI SOL DO. Some of the more common melodic skips are shown in the examples below.

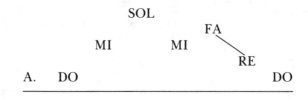

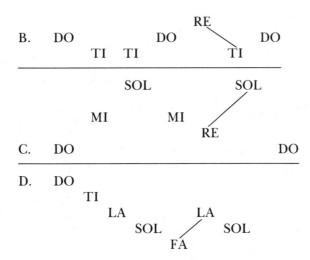

Practice Progressions

Singing the practice progressions shown below can provide help in learning to execute skips other than DO MI SOL.

1. *ASCENDING*

RE
DO   DO
TI   TI
LA   LA
SOL   SOL
FA   FA
MI   MI
RE
DO

DESCENDING
DO
TI
LA   LA
SOL   SOL
FA   FA
MI   MI
RE   RE
DO   DO
TI

2. ASCENDING

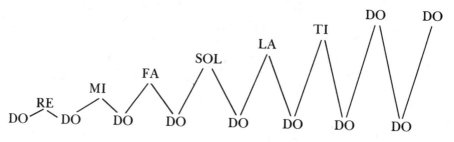

DESCENDING

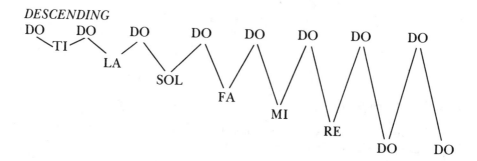

Practice Melodies for Skips Other Than DO MI SOL (Off Staff)

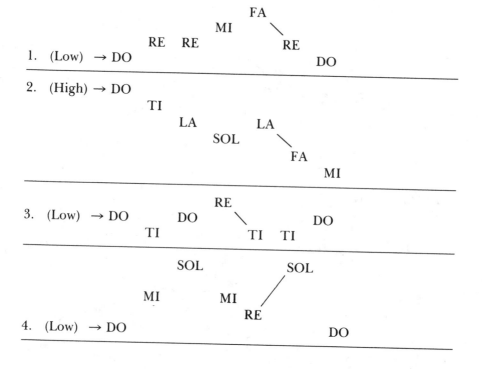

5. (High) → DO

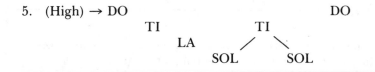

6. (High) → DO

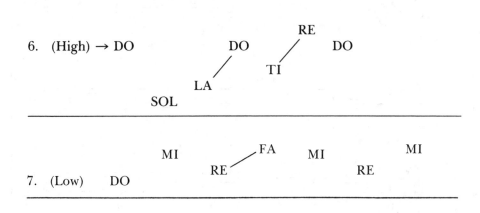

7. (Low)   DO

Writing Skips Other Than DO MI SOL on Staff

Skips other than DO MI SOL will also show intervening lines and spaces when written on the staff:

DO MI SOL MI FA RE DO

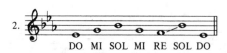

DO MI SOL MI RE SOL DO

DO TI TI DO RE TI DO

QUESTIONS

12. In the staves below write the notes in their appropriate places according to the syllables given (initial DO is shown in place).

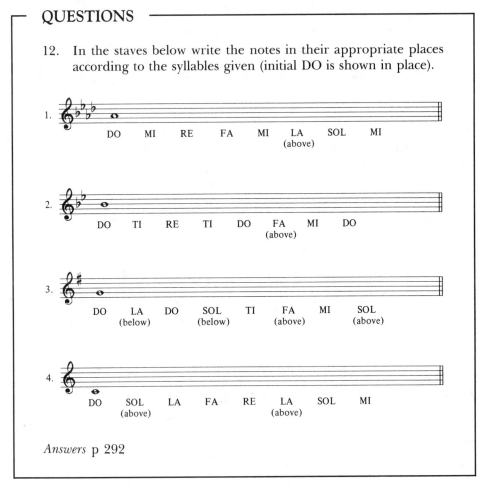

Answers p 292

Practice Melodies on Staff for Skips Other Than DO MI SOL

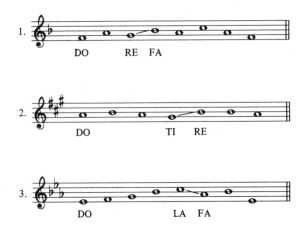

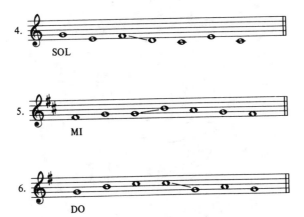

For additional practice in singing with syllables, try the Practice Melodies (PM) and songs on the pages listed below. These melodies/songs contain only the simple rhythms introduced in Chapter 2.

Stepwise: p. 20 ("Old Hundred"); p. 29 (PM 1, 2, and 3); p. 25 (PM 1, 2, and 4); p. 20 (PM 1, 2, and 3); p. 22 (PM 1, 2, and 3).
DO MI SOL Skip: p. 149 (PM 3); p. 133 (PM 3 and 4); p. 155 (PM 1, 2, and 3).
Other Skips: p. 23 ("Sweet Betsy"); p. 25 ("Good Night"); p. 27 ("Go Tell Aunt Rhody"); p. 29 ("Lovely Evening"); p. 30 ("Riddle Song").

See also the Practice Melodies and songs on pp. 135–136, 137–138, 145–146, 147, and 151–158.

Curwen Hand Signals

John Curwen, a nineteenth-century English musician, developed a system of hand signals for practice in learning to sing scale syllables. These have seen widespread use in many countries, including the United States.

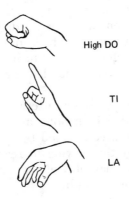

High DO

TI

LA

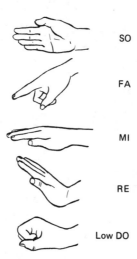

SO

FA

MI

RE

Low DO

IMPROVING VOCAL PERFORMANCE

Attention to the following may prove helpful in improving tone quality when singing:

>   *Posture.* In a sitting position both feet should be flat on the floor, with back reasonably straight but not rigid.
>   *Breathing.* Breathe from the diaphragm. To aid in this, the following simple exercise is suggested.
>   a. Encircle the lowest rib with middle fingers of each hand touching in front, thumbs pointing toward the back. *Inhale,* forcing the diaphragm to expand and push the middle fingers apart. *Exhale,* allowing the diaphragm to "deflate" and the middle fingers to resume touching. Repeat inhaling and exhaling several times.
>   b. Inhale deeply as before, then exhale on a comfortable pitch, a little at a time, conserving the breath so as to sustain the tone as long as possible. In a group setting several different tones may be assigned to produce harmony when sounded on the exhalation.
>   This kind of diaphragmatic breathing enables the breath control necessary for good musical phrasing.
>   *Diction.* Clear diction demands that words be formed carefully on the front of the mouth in what may feel, initially, like an exaggerated lip position to the new singer. "Over-enunciation" seems an appropriate way to describe what is recommended for better diction.

Those who feel threatened by the presence of high notes may take some comfort in the suggestion that high notes are more easily sounded when the singer uses a "lighter" tone accompanied by a mental image of approaching the tone from above rather than trying to reach up to it. (Raising the chin won't help at all!) Tension may also affect tone quality. Try the following simple relaxing exercises for unwinding:

A. Tighten the entire body to a very stiff position—like a robot. Hold the position for two seconds, then loosen and go limp all over—like a rag doll. Repeat several times.
B. Stand with arms raised overhead. Drop one part of the body at a time in the following sequence (one count each for a total of eight counts):
    1. left wrist
    2. right wrist
    3. left forearm
    4. right forearm
    5. left upper arm
    6. right upper arm
    7. head
    8. torso (hang loosely, head down)
Accompany with a descending scale, one movement for each tone of the scale.

Vocal Warm-up

The voice, as well as other parts of the body, needs warming up before use. Try the following simple vocal warm-up exercise:

Ascend as high as desired using each vowel sound in its pure form, then insert *b*, *d* or other initial consonant before vowel sound and proceed as above.

Phrasing

A *phrase* may be defined as a "short musical thought." Basically, it is a portion of the melody. A complete melody is made up of numerous phrases.

Phrases in music may be compared to phrases in language and as such may be of varying lengths and punctuated by pausing places known as *cadences*. (See "Cadences," p. 214). In performance, these musical cadences frequently provide possible breathing places to facilitate a smoother flow in the process of singing or playing.

Proper phrasing—vital to good musical interpretation—can be enhanced through attention to breath control (see p. 98). Breath intake in too many places produces a choppy, fragmented result similar to that sometimes heard in schools. For example, during the singing of "America," frequently, children may be heard taking random breaths between word syllables such as "Sweet land of lib-(breath)-er-ty. . . ." Erratic breathing patterns that interfere with good phrasing tend to detract from the overall beauty of the performance.

As an aid to performers, breathing places for some musical selections are indicated by a particular symbol such as an apostrophe (') or may be in the form of long curved lines over each phrase designated to be executed in a single breath.

QUESTIONS

13. A phrase may be defined as a _____.
14. A complete melody is made up of _____ _____.
15. Pausing places in music are known as _____.
16. Proper phrasing may be enhanced through attention to

_____.

Answers p 292

Chapter Five

Scales and Keys

INTERVALS

The word *interval* refers to the musical distance between two tones. The distance from C to the adjacent D (DO-RE) is an interval of a 2nd:

From C to the E above (DO-MI) would be an interval of a 3rd:

When reckoning intervals, the primary (first) tone is counted as *one*:

Intervals may also be reckoned downward. From C to the E below is an interval of a 6th:

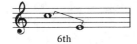

Depending on how they occur in the music, intervals may be referred to as *melodic* or *harmonic*. A *melodic* interval is determined by counting the musical distance from one tone to the next in a horizontal melody line:

An *harmonic* interval is determined by counting the musical distance between tones arranged vertically in chord form and sounded simultaneously:

In addition to numerical labels, intervals may also be referred to by other designations such as *diminished, augmented, minor, perfect* and *major*, depending on their content.

QUESTIONS

1. The musical distance between tones is called an _____.
2. From C to the F above is an interval of a _____.
3. From B to the G below is an interval of a _____.
4. Identify each of the intervals shown below by number:

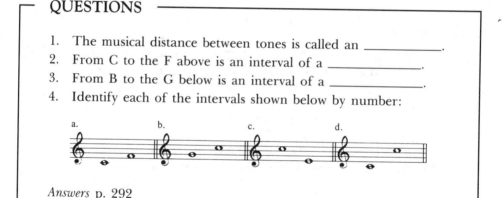

Answers p. 292

MAJOR SCALES

In Western music, one of the most frequently heard scales is the *major scale*. Music that consists mainly of major scale tones with DO as the tonal center is said to be in a *major key*. Each key has its own scale. Scales represent prescribed orders of pitch relationships or intervals. The established order for the major scale is:

> *half* steps between the 3rd and 4th tones (MI and FA) and between the 7th and 8th tones (TI and DO) of the given scale,
> *whole* steps between all others:

```
                      ½ step            ½ step
        1   2   3 /\ 4   5   6   7 /\ 8
        DO  RE  MI  FA  SOL LA  TI  DO
```

QUESTIONS

5. The most frequently heard scale in Western music is the
    _____ scale. The tonal center (or keynote) for this
    scale is always _____.

6. In any given major scale half steps must occur between the
    _____ and _____ tones and between the
    _____ and _____ tones of the scale.

7. The syllable names of the 3rd and 4th tones of the major scale
    are _____ and _____.

8. The syllable names of the 7th and 8th tones of the major scale
    are _____ and _____.

Answers p. 293

Whole Steps and Half Steps (Piano Keyboard)

Whole steps and half steps are more easily understood when viewed on
the piano keyboard. The illustration shown below is that of a complete piano
keyboard consisting of 88 black and white keys arranged in successively repeated patterns:

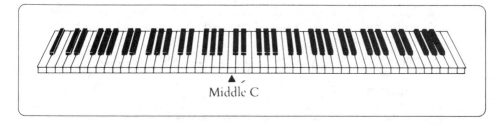

Middle C

From a white key to its adjacent black key is a *half step* interval:

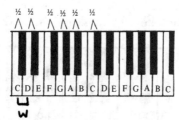

A black key occurring between two white keys means that there is a *whole step*
between the two white keys:

Where no black key is present, there is a *half step* between the adjacent white keys. Note this occurrence between the notes E and F and B and C in the keyboard below:

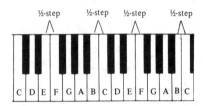

QUESTIONS

9. The piano keyboard contains a total of _____ keys.

10. From any white key to the adjacent black key is an interval of a _____ step.

11. When a black key appears between two white keys there is an interval of a _____ step between the two white keys.

12. When there is *no* black key between two adjacent white keys there is an interval of a _____ step between the two white keys. On the piano keyboard this interval occurs normally between the notes _____ and _____ as well as between the notes _____ and _____.

Answers p. 293

Note that the black keys appear in recurring groups of twos and threes throughout the keyboard. C is the white key located immediately to the *left* of *each* group of *two* black keys. F is the white key located immediately to the *left* of *each* group of *three* black keys throughout the keyboard.

↑
Middle C

A common reference point on any piano keyboard is the note *middle C*, located at the left of the two black keys nearest to and slightly left of the manufacturer's name in the center of the keyboard.

Mnf. Name

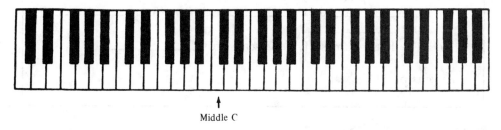

Middle C

On the treble clef it is written:

Middle C

On the bass clef:

The C Major Scale

In the scale of C—played on all white keys—the half steps and whole steps fall naturally in their prescribed positions, that is, half steps between the 3rd and 4th and 7th and 8th tones of the scale and whole steps between all others.

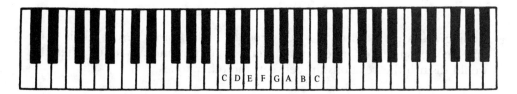

1   2   3   4   5   6   7   8

DO RE MI FA SOL LA TI DO

QUESTIONS

13. When playing the scale of C one does not play any _____ keys.

14. On the piano keyboard there is no black key between _____ and _____ or between _____ and _____.

15. The letter names of the C scale are _____.

Answers p. 293

Scales in Sharp Keys

The G Major Scale   Scales in keys other than C require alterations of certain tones in order to accommodate the whole and half step pattern prescribed for a major scale. Such alterations are accomplished through the use of *sharps* or *flats* depending on the key. In the scale of G, for example, the whole steps presently existing between the 7th and 8th tones (F–G) must be reduced to a half step, while the present half step between the 6th and 7th tones (E–F) must be increased to a whole step. (In this key the required half step interval between the 3rd and 4th tones falls naturally in the proper place—between B and C.)

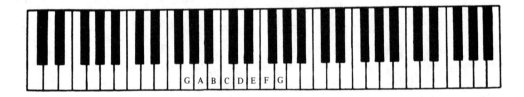

Adding a sharp to the note F will produce both desired results. This is the only choice, since key notes may never be altered; and any other alteration would disturb the relationship between the other tones.

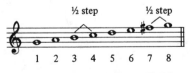

DO RE MI FA SOL LA TI DO

A sharp (♯) placed before a note indicates that the note is to be sounded a half step higher. On the piano keyboard this means to play the black key directly to the right of the white key:

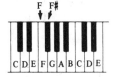

When playing the scale of G on the piano, note that the black key F♯ must be played in place of the white key F.

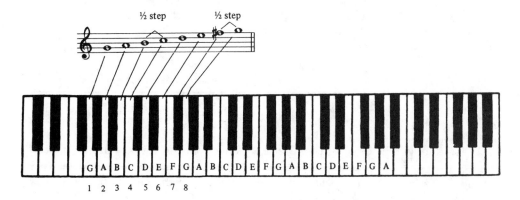

In scales containing many sharps such as F♯,

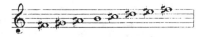

if no black key exists for the given note, the adjacent white key must be played:

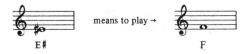

Note in the foregoing alterations that each sharp is placed on the same line or space as the note it is intended to affect, immediately *preceding* the note; however, when identified the letter name is spoken first followed by the word "sharp": "E sharp."

QUESTIONS

16. The scale may be written without alterations when starting on the note _____.

17. Notes may be altered through the use of _____ and
_____.

18. When any tone is altered, this alteration changes the size of the _____ between it and its adjacent tone.

19. The interval between F♯ and G is a _____ step.

20. The interval distance between C♯ and D is a _____ step.

21. On the staff below place each of the notes indicated by the letter names shown, making certain to place the ♯ symbols in their proper places:

F♯   D♯   A♯

Answers p. 293

In a longer piece of music, the sharps necessary to the key are *not* placed in front of the notes every time they occur in the piece (that would be very untidy!); rather they are placed on the staff next to the clef sign where they become known as the *key signature*.

In the key of G the one sharp in the key signature affects every F throughout that piece of music:

Scales and keys having sharps in the key signature are G, D, A, E, B, F♯ and C♯. In this sequence, the number of sharps added increases by one each time. Note the interval of a 5th between successive letters.

1♯ = Key of G	5♯s = Key of B
2♯s = Key of D	6♯s = Key of F♯
3♯s = Key of A	7♯s = Key of C♯
4♯s = Key of E	

QUESTIONS

22. The black key directly above F is _____.
23. The black key directly above C is _____.
24. A _____ is a sign used to denote a black key directly above a given white key.
25. The group of one or more sharps found next to the clef sign is known as the _____ _____.
26. In a key signature of one sharp, the key would be _____ major.
27. There is an interval of a _____ between each successive sharp key letter name.

Answers p. 293

28. Below are several different starting tones for major scales that contain sharps, accompanied by illustrations of keyboards for helpful reference. Do the following for each scale in the order suggested:
    a. Insert all the notes of the scale in ascending order; for example:

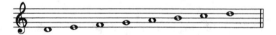

    b. Mark the location of the half steps; for example:

    c. Insert the sharps where necessary to accommodate the whole/half step prescribed major scale pattern; for example:

Note: Each sharp must be placed on the same line or space as its affected note immediately *preceding* the note.

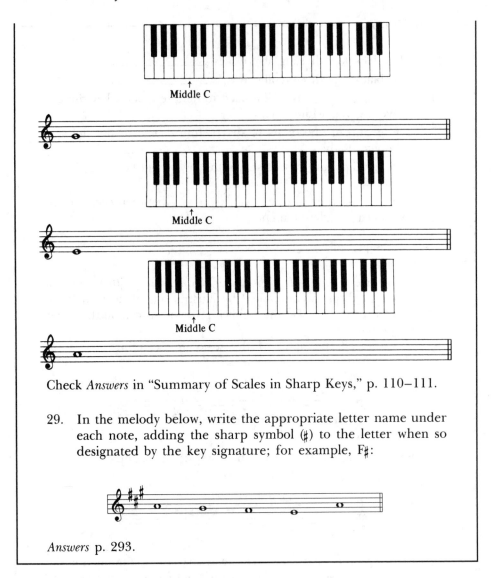

Check *Answers* in "Summary of Scales in Sharp Keys," p. 110–111.

29. In the melody below, write the appropriate letter name under each note, adding the sharp symbol (♯) to the letter when so designated by the key signature; for example, F♯:

Answers p. 293.

SUMMARY OF SCALES IN SHARP (♯) KEYS

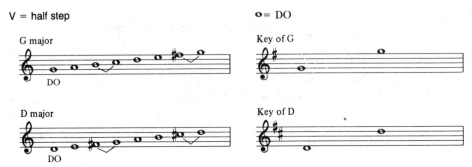

Scales in Flat Keys

The F Major Scale   In some keys the flat symbol (♭) must be used for needed alterations of certain tones in order to maintain the proper order of whole and half step relationships that characterize a major scale. In the key of F (shown below) there is a whole step between the 3rd and 4th tones (A and B) that must be reduced to a half step.

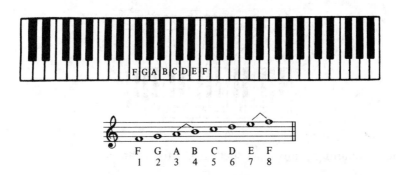

Placing a *flat* (♭) in front of B will provide the required half step interval while at the same time increasing the existing half step interval between the 4th and 5th tones to a required whole step. In this key the prescribed half step interval between the 7th and 8th tones (E and F) occurs naturally in the proper place.

A flat (♭) placed before a note indicates that the note is to be sounded a half step lower. On the piano keyboard this means to play the adjacent black key located directly to the left of the white key.

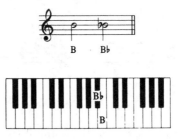

When playing the scale of F on the piano, the black key B♭ must be played in place of the white key B:

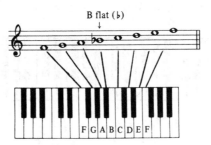

In scales containing many flats such as G♭, for example,

if no black key exists for the given note, the adjacent white key must be played:

Cb   means to play →   B

Note that the flat symbol is placed on the same line or space as the note it is intended to affect immediately preceding the note; however, when identified the letter name is spoken first, followed by the word "flat," as, "C flat."

QUESTIONS

30. The scale of F contains one altered tone which is _____.
31. The black key directly below B is _____.
32. One flat in the key signature means that DO is on

    _____.

33. The interval between B and B♭ is a _____ step.
34. The interval between E and F is a _____ step.
35. On the staff below place each of the notes shown by their letter names, making certain to place the flat symbols in their proper places:

    Db   Eb   Bb

Answers p. 293

In a longer piece of music, the flats necessary to the key are not placed in front of the notes every time they occur in the piece; rather, they are placed at the beginning next to the clef sign where they are known as the *key signature*. In the key of F the one flat in the key signature will affect every B appearing in that piece of music:

Scales and keys having flats in the key signature are F, B♭, E♭, A♭, D♭, G♭ and C♭. In this sequence the number of flats increases by one each time. Note the interval of a 4th between successive letters.

1♭ = Key of F	5♭s = Key of D♭
2♭s = Key of B♭	6♭s = Key of G♭
3♭s = Key of E♭	7♭s = Key of C♭
4♭s = Key of A♭	

QUESTIONS

36. Four flats in the key signature means that the music is written in the key of _____ major and that DO is on

_____.

37. The key of C contains _____ flats.

38. The key of E♭ contains _____ flats in the key signature and DO is on _____.

39. There is an interval of a _____ between each successive flat key letter name.

40. Below are several different starting tones for major scales that contain flats, accompanied by illustrations of keyboards for helpful reference. Do the following for each scale in the order suggested:

    a. Insert all the notes of the scale in ascending order; for example:

    b. Mark the location of the half steps; for example:

    c. Insert the flats where necessary to accommodate the whole/half step prescribed major scale pattern; for example:

Note: Each flat must be placed on the same line or space as its affected note immediately *preceding* the note.

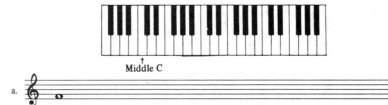

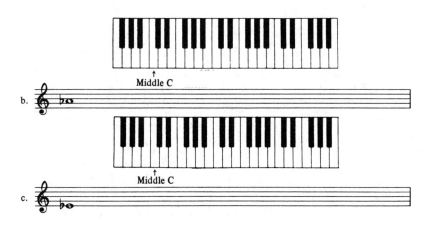

Check *Answers* in "Summary of Scales in Flat Keys," below.

41. In the melody below, write the appropriate letter name under each note, adding the flat symbol (♭) to the letter when so designated by the key signature; for example, D♭.

Answers p. 293

SUMMARY OF SCALES IN FLAT (♭) KEYS

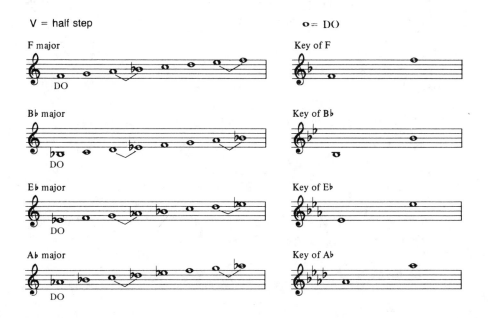

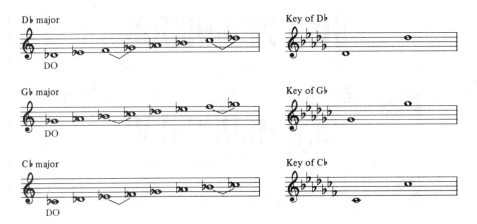

Finding DO from Key Signatures

Although the presence of the sharps and flats found in key signatures has been accounted for in the study of scale construction, certainly it is not necessary to build scales before being able to locate DO or to determine the names of keys. DO may be found easily from any given key signature as follows:

A. **With sharps.** When there are sharps (♯) in the key signature, look for the *last* sharp to the right—the one farthest away from the clef sign. Call the last sharp by the syllable name TI or the scale number (7) and count up one place to DO using ascending scale sequence (TI–DO) or numbers (7–8). If TI falls on a space, then DO will fall on the line above TI:

If TI falls on a line, DO will fall on the space above TI:

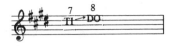

The same procedure also applies to finding DO on the bass clef when there are sharps in the key signature:

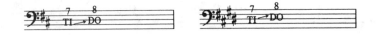

QUESTIONS

42. If TI falls on a space, DO will fall on the _____ (line, space) above TI.

43. If TI is on a line, DO will be on the space _____ (above, below) TI.

44. If TI is on the third space, DO will be on the _____ _____.

45. In the key signatures shown below mark the location of DO with an X:

Answers p. 294

B. With flats. When there are flats (♭) in the key signature, look for the *last* flat to the right—the one farthest away from the clef sign. Call the last flat by its syllable name FA or its scale number (4) and count down to DO using the notes in the descending scale (FA MI RE DO) or the numbers (4 3 2 1).

The same procedure also applies to finding DO on the bass clef when there are flats in the key signature:

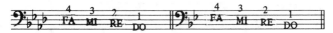

In key signatures containing more than one flat, the *next* to the last flat is always on DO.

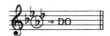

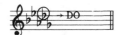

QUESTIONS

46. In key signatures containing flats, DO is located by calling the last flat _____.

47. When there are two or more flats in the key signature, DO may also be found on the _____ _____
_____ _____ _____.

48. In the key signatures shown below, mark the location of DO with an X:

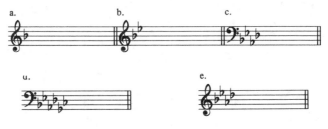

Answers p. 294

C. **With no sharps or flats.** When there are no sharps or flats in the key signature, DO in the treble clef is always on the third space or the first leger line *below* the staff:

In the bass clef, when there are no sharps or flats in the key signature, DO is always on the second space or the first line *above* the staff:

QUESTIONS

49. Locate DO in the following key signatures (mark with an X):

Answers p. 294

Naming Keys

With Sharps   Locating DO is also an aid in determining the key of any given song, since the letter name of the line or space upon which DO falls is also that of the key.

When DO falls on E the name of the key is E:

When DO falls on G the name of the key is G:

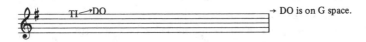

It should be noted that when there are six or seven sharps in the key signature, the line or space upon which DO falls *already shows a sharp* on it in the key signature. When this occurs, the name of the key must also include the word "sharp," for example:

Key of F♯   Key of C♯
(DO is on F♯)   (DO is on C♯)

QUESTIONS

50. The name of any key may be determined by first locating

    _____.

51. The line or space upon which _____ falls is the name of the key.

52. When DO falls on the fourth line of the treble clef, the name of the key is _____.

53. When DO falls on the _____ _____ of the treble clef the name of the key is E.

54. Locate DO with an X and name the key in the following key signatures:

Answers p. 294

The same rule for naming keys also applies to the bass clef, that is, the line or space upon which DO falls is the name of the *key*. As noted previously, the lowest line of the bass clef is *G* and all other letter names of lines and spaces must be reckoned accordingly in alphabetical order:

Key of D

QUESTIONS

55. In the bass clef, when DO falls on the third line, the name of the key is _____.

56. In sharp keys, DO is located by calling the _____ _____ TI.

57. The first line of the bass clef is _____ (letter name).

Answers p. 294

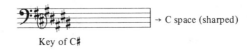

Key of C♯

In the above example, DO is on the second space C in the bass clef. Since there is a sharp on the C space in the key signature, the name of the key shown would be C♯.

QUESTIONS

58. What is the name of the key in this example?

59. C is found on the _____ space of the bass clef.

60. Locate DO and name the key in the following key signatures (mark with an X):

Answers p. 294

With Flats   Determining the names of keys having flats in the key signature is done in the same way as for those containing sharps—that is, by simply locating DO and naming the line or space upon which DO falls:

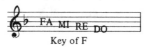

Key of F

In the example above, the last flat (FA) is on the third line, thus DO is in the first space. The name of the first space of the treble clef is F, thus the example shown is in the key of F.

The same rule applies to the bass clef. In the example below, FA is on the second line, DO is on the space below the staff. The name of that space is F; thus this example is in the key of F:

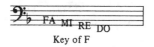

Key of F

QUESTIONS

61.   In the above example, DO is on the _____ _____ the staff.
62.   The letter name of the location of DO in the above example is _____.
63.   The above example is in the key of _____.

Answers p. 294

If the line or space upon which DO falls shows a flat in the key signature, the name of the key must include the word "flat." In the key signature of two flats shown below, DO is located on the third line, which already has been flatted in the key signature:

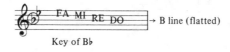

Key of B♭

When this occurs, the key must be called by its letter name, plus the word "flat" or the symbol for flat (♭) if written: B♭ (B flat), A♭ (A flat), and so on.

┌─ QUESTIONS ───────────────────────────

64. In the example above, the name of the key is _____.
65. DO in the same example is located on the _____
_____ of the treble clef.

Answers p. 295
└──

The same rule applies to the bass clef. If the note upon which DO falls has previously been flatted in the key signature, the letter name of the key must have the word "flat" added to it:

Key of A♭

In the above example, DO is located on the first space. Note that there is a flat on the first space in the key signature. The name of the first space in the bass clef is A; thus the name of the key would be A♭ (A flat).

┌─ QUESTIONS ───────────────────────────

66. In the key of A♭, DO is located in the _____ space of the bass clef.

67. To find DO with flats, call the last flat to the right _____.

Answers p. 295
└──

Naming Keys With no Sharps or Flats   When there are neither sharps nor flats in the key signature in the *treble clef* DO is always on the third space or the first line below the staff, and the name of the key is C:

DO
DO   Key of C

In the *bass clef* when there are no sharps or flats in the key signature, DO is always on the second space or the first line above the staff and the name of the key is C:

DO
DO   Key of C

QUESTIONS

68. Locate DO with an X in the following signatures:

69. Locate DO with an X and name the key in the following signatures:

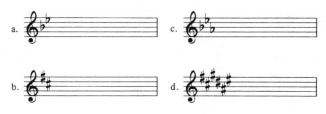

a.　　　　　c.

b.　　　　　d.

Answers p. 295

Circle of Keys

Key signature relationships may be graphically summarized in the *circle of keys* shown below. Starting from the twelve o'clock position with the key of C (no sharps or flats) and reading clockwise, note that the interval between the sharp keys in sequence is that of an ascending 5th. Reading counterclockwise from the key of C, note that the interval between the flat keys in sequence is an ascending 4th.

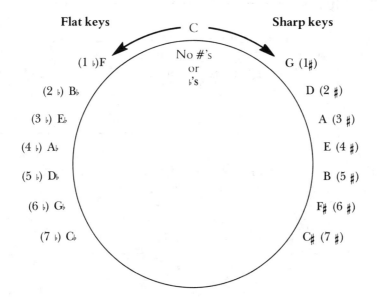

Flat keys　　　　　C　　　　　Sharp keys

No #'s
or
♭'s

(1 ♭)F　　　　　　　　　　　G (1♯)

(2 ♭) B♭　　　　　　　　　　D (2 ♯)

(3 ♭) E♭　　　　　　　　　　A (3 ♯)

(4 ♭) A♭　　　　　　　　　　E (4 ♯)

(5 ♭) D♭　　　　　　　　　　B (5 ♯)

(6 ♭) G♭　　　　　　　　　　F♯ (6 ♯)

(7 ♭) C♭　　　　　　　　　　C♯ (7 ♯)

Placement of Sharps and Flats on Staff in Key Signatures

In writing key signatures on the staff, the placement of sharps or flats follows an established order that cannot be altered. The first sharp is always placed on the F line. Note in the example below, F in the treble clef will fall on the fifth line, while in the bass clef F will fall on the fourth line:

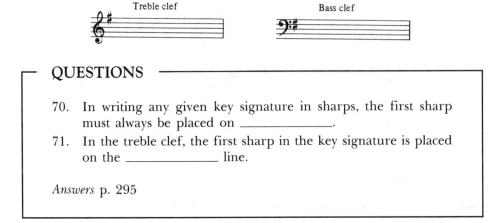

Treble clef   Bass clef

QUESTIONS

70. In writing any given key signature in sharps, the first sharp must always be placed on _____.

71. In the treble clef, the first sharp in the key signature is placed on the _____ line.

Answers p. 295

In writing a key signature of two sharps, the first sharp must be placed on the F line; the second sharp must be placed on the C space:

Treble clef   Bass clef

QUESTIONS

72. In the bass clef, the second sharp is placed on the C space, which is the _____ space of the staff.

73. In the treble clef, C is located on the _____ space.

Answers p. 295

In writing a key signature of three sharps, the first sharp must be placed on the F line, the second sharp on the C space, and the third sharp on the high G space:

Treble clef   Bass clef

QUESTIONS

74. The order of the first three sharps in a key signature is: (1) _____, (2) _____, (3) _____.

75. The sharp on G must always be placed in the _____ position.

Answers p. 295

There may be as many as seven sharps in a key signature, placed as follows:

Treble clef

Bass clef

The order is F C G D A E B on both clefs. This order cannot be altered.

Note that the letter sequence F C G D A E B moves by 5s in the musical alphabet: counting the first sharp *F* as one, the next sharp C is five letters away from F; the third sharp G is five letters away from C, etc. Remembering the name of the first sharp (F) in the sequence will enable finding all the others by simply counting up five letters from the given starting letter in the musical alphabet.

QUESTIONS

76. When there are four sharps in a key signature, the letter name of the fourth sharp is _____.

77. Each sharp key is _____ alphabet letters apart from the next in sequence.

Answers p. 295

In placing flats in flat key signatures, the first flat must be placed on the B line:

Treble clef

Bass clef

┌─ QUESTIONS ───┐

78. The B line of the treble clef staff is the _____ line.
79. The B line of the bass clef staff is the _____ line.

Answers p. 296

└───┘

When there are two flats, the first flat must be placed on the B line, the second flat on the E space:

┌─ QUESTIONS ───┐

80. In the treble clef, the second flat E is placed in the _____
     space.
81. In the bass clef, the first flat is placed on the _____
     line and the second flat on the _____ space.

Answers p. 296

└───┘

There may be as many as seven flats in a key signature, placed as follows:

The order is B E A D G C F. Note that the order is exactly the reverse of that for placement of sharps. The letter sequence B E A D G C F moves by 4s in the musical alphabet: counting B, the first flat as one, the next flat E is four away from B; the third flat A is four away from E, etc. Remembering the name of the first flat in a key signature enables one to find all the others simply by counting up the musical alphabet in 4s. The starting letter must always be reckoned as *one*.

┌─ QUESTIONS ───┐

82. In a key signature with five flats, the last flat will be placed on
     _____ (letter name).
83. A key signature of four flats will look like this:

84. Each flat key is _____ alphabet letters apart from the next in sequence.

Answers p. 296

In the staves below, write in the appropriate sharps or flats in their designated places according to the number specified (note clefs).

1. 4 sharps   *write scale*   1.

2. 2 flats   2.

3. 1 flat   3.

4. 5 sharps   4.

5. 6 flats   5.

6. 4 flats   6.

7. 7 sharps   7.

8. 5 sharps   8.

Check *Answers* with "Key Summary" on pp. 128–129.

KEY SUMMARY

Sharp Keys

(**o** = location of DO)

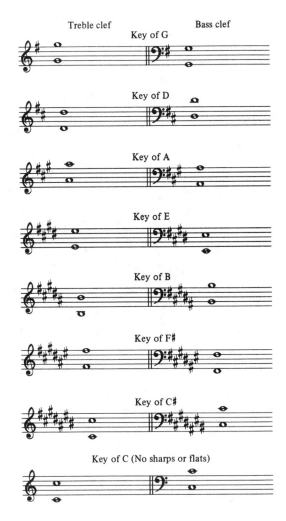

KEY SUMMARY

Flat Keys

(**o** = location of DO)

TRANSPOSITION

Transposition simply means shifting a song from one key into a different key—
a process that may be prescribed for various reasons. For example, not all
instruments can play in all keys. Many harmonicas are limited to one key;
certain Autoharps to four. (See Chapter 10.) Although ukuleles and guitars
may be played in any key, the finger positions for various chords in some
keys may prove awkward and difficult for the nonprofessional. For singers,
certain songs may extend out of a singer's vocal range. Transposing such
songs to a different key can facilitate improved performance.

Several methods may be used for transposing, depending on personal
preference. One simple way is with the use of scale syllables as shown below.
Whichever way is chosen, the most important first step is to identify correctly
the key and starting tone of the song to be transposed. In the following example, the given song is in the key of D, with DO located on the first space
below the staff (or fourth line).

To transpose using scale syllables; do the following:

1. Determine the name of the starting note from the key signature
   shown, then write the syllable names under the notes of the song:

Do   mi   sol   mi sol   la   sol   mi sol   la   sol   mi sol   etc.

2. Write the names of the same syllables in succession under a blank staff containing the desired new key signature. (For this example the key of F was chosen as the new key, with DO located on the first space (or fifth line):

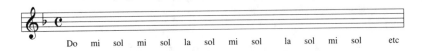

Do   mi   sol   mi   sol   la   sol   mi   sol   la   sol   mi   sol   etc

3. Locate DO in the new key, then place each note on the proper line or space above the corresponding syllable name:

Do   mi   sol   mi sol   la   sol   mi sol   la   sol   mi sol   etc.

To transpose by interval, determine the starting note of the new key desired, then place the notes on the staff in the same interval order as those in the given key; for example, in the song excerpt shown above, the second note is an interval of a *major 3rd* away from the first note; the third note is an interval of a *minor 3rd* away from the second note, etc.

Using either of these methods (and others not included here) songs can be transposed from any one key into any other key. Simply insert the appropriate key signature for the new key desired, locate DO in that key, determine the name of the starting tone, and proceed as above. (See also "Transposing Chords," p. 210.)

Chapter Six

Playing Melody Instruments

Music theory, such as that found on the foregoing pages, is best understood when it can be applied in practice. The following materials for piano, resonator bells, and recorder are intended to reinforce various musical learnings and to provide opportunities for acquiring basic skills on the instruments.

A single recorder can play only one tone at a time. A piano can play several tones simultaneously; therefore it may be considered a chording instrument as well as a melody instrument. It is being included here under melody instruments because it is the intent to deal only with that particular function—playing melody. (Chording on piano may be found in Chapter 9.)

PIANO (RIGHT HAND)

As noted previously, the piano keyboard has eighty-eight black and white keys arranged in repeated patterns, with the black keys recurring in groups of twos and threes. In each complete pattern of seven white and five black keys, twelve different notes are possible.

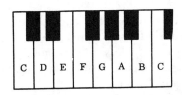

It has been noted that the white key immediately to the left of each group of *two* black keys is always C, while the white key immediately to the left of each group of *three* black keys is always F. This remains the same throughout the entire keyboard.

↑
Middle C

The location of specific Fs and Cs as well as all other notes is dependent upon where they appear on the staff and which clef is used. For example, the notes shown below are written in the same location on each staff but using different clefs. The note on the bass clef first space is A, whereas the note on the same space in the treble clef is F. Observe that the first space bass clef note is located much lower on the piano keyboard than the first space treble clef note:

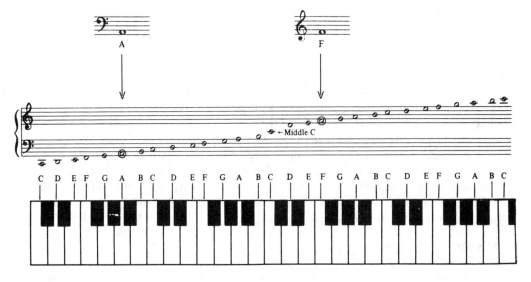

When playing the piano, the right hand usually plays from the treble clef, the left hand from the bass clef.

Playing Position

The player should be seated far enough away from the keyboard to allow the body to bend slightly forward to accommodate the reach, with shoulders reflecting a comfortable sitting position—not rigid. Fingers should be curved, with the wrists held slightly higher than the fingers and not allowed to sag. Hands should remain on a fairly even level, with the fingers kept close to the keys at all times, avoiding the necessity for using the whole hand to execute the striking motion.

As an aid to reading, the eye should be looking slightly beyond the immediate note being played to facilitate the transition from that note to the next without hesitation. This will help to maintain the steady beat.

Right Hand Practice Melodies (Five Note)

The following melodies contain a maximum of five notes and are included here for introductory practice since they may be easily adapted to playing with the five fingers of the right hand. Right hand fingers are numbered as follows:

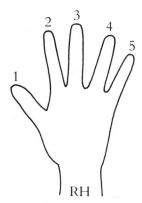

Fingering for some of the tunes has been marked. In others it has been left unmarked to afford practice in selecting the appropriate fingering.

Key of C

MERRILY WE ROLL ALONG

Mer - ri - ly we roll a - long, roll a - long, roll a - long,

Mer - ri - ly we roll a - long o'er the deep blue sea.

DRINK TO ME ONLY WITH THINE EYES (excerpt)

MY LORD WHAT A MORNING (excerpt)

The following simple practice melodies are in different keys from those shown above. Observe that any note shown flatted or sharped in the key signature must be played flatted or sharped each time it occurs in the melody.

Key of F

Note flat (♭) in key signature.

LOVE SOMEBODY

Folk Song

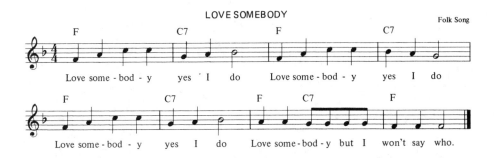

Love some - bod - y   yes I do   Love some - bod - y   yes I do

Love some - bod - y   yes I do   Love some - bod - y but I won't say who.

SOME FOLKS (excerpt)

STEPHEN FOSTER

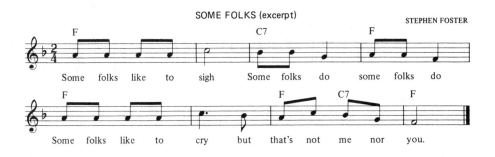

Some   folks   like   to   sigh   Some   folks   do   some   folks   do

Some   folks   like   to   cry   but   that's   not   me   nor   you.

DEAF WOMAN'S COURTSHIP

Folk Song

Key of D

Note sharps (♯) in key signature.

WHISTLE, DAUGHTER

American Folk Song

1. "Whis - tle, daugh - ter, whis - tle, and you shall have a cow."
2. "Whis - tle, daugh - ter, whis - tle, and you shall have a pig."

"I can't whis - tle, moth - er, be - cause I don't know how."
"I can't whis - tle, moth - er, be - cause I am too big."

3. Whistle, daughter, whistle, and you shall have a man.
(WHISTLE)   I just found out I can.

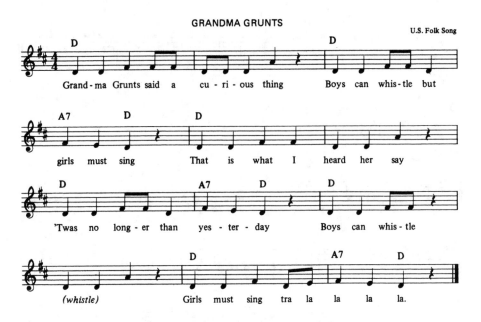

GRANDMA GRUNTS

U.S. Folk Song

Additional Practice Melodies (PM) and songs suitable for playing five-finger melodies in various keys may be found in the recorder section on the following pages:

p. 145 (PM 1–5)
p. 146 songs
p. 147 (PM 1–3) and songs
p. 148 song
p. 150 (PM 1, 2, and 4)
p. 153 (PM 1–3)
p. 155 (PM 3)
p. 158 (PM 1 and 2)

RESONATOR BELLS

Resonator bells are single blocks of wood or other material with a metal bar attached over a small opening to allow the sound to resonate. Each bell is tuned to a different pitch, the letter name of which appears on the bar. Sound is produced by striking the metal bar with a hard rubber mallet, grasping the handle firmly, then flicking the wrist so that the ball of the mallet bounces back upward after striking the bell. When arranged in proper order, resonator bells resemble a piano keyboard, with black and white key patterns corresponding to those of the piano.

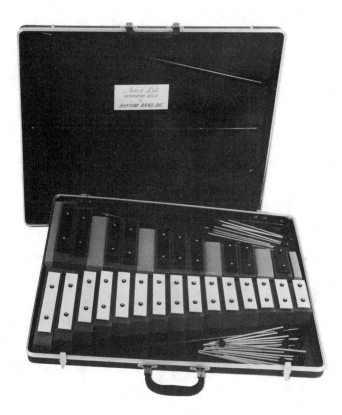

Although resonator bells are commonly viewed as a melody instrument (and as such are being included here), they may also be used to produce chords by sounding selected bells simultaneously (see "Chords on Resonator Bells," p. 282). These bells may be handled and played separately, since the blocks are not attached.

Any of the melodies suggested for right hand piano on the foregoing pages as well as other selected song material throughout the book may be played on resonator bells.

ACTIVITIES

1. Arrange individual bells in proper sequence for illustrating various scales and modes (whole tone, pentatonic, blues, etc.). Improvise original melodies on the selected bells.
2. Try playing "Swing Low," "Old MacDonald," and other pentatonic tunes by ear, using black keys only (see p. 190).
3. Select bells D E F♯ G B and create a tune using those five tones only. Add rhythm.
4. Rearrange six bells from their traditional positions into a random sequence and play the resulting tune. Add rhythm.

5. Use bells in place of voice to sound the descants to songs shown on pages following page 219 or to create original descants to play with songs of your choice (see "Creating Harmony," p. 215).

6. Use bells in place of voice to sound chord roots of selected songs while group sings the song or plays it on a melody instrument (see "Creating Harmony," p. 215).

7. If more than one set of bells is available, use one for playing melody, the other for sounding chords, descants, chord roots, etc.

8. Select appropriate bells for playing chords to accompany songs of choice. Select those using I, IV, and V7 chords only at first (see "Chords on Resonator Bells," p. 282).

9. Create an arrangement of a song of choice to play using bells, recorder, Autoharp, and rhythm instruments.

RECORDER

The *recorder* is referred to as a *melody instrument* because its chief function is to play melody rather than harmony. Classified as a *wind instrument*, the recorder is played in the same way as some of the traditional orchestral wind instruments — by blowing into an opening to produce the sound while covering holes with the fingers to vary the pitch.

Recorders come in various sizes and ranges — soprano, alto, tenor and bass. The larger the size, the lower the sound. Several recorders playing together can produce harmony.

THE SOPRANO RECORDER

Holding Position

The first three fingers of the left hand are used to play the *upper* set of openings — those nearest to the mouthpiece. The thumb of the left hand covers the opening on the underside of the instrument. The little finger of the left hand is not used at all. The fingers of the *right* hand play the *lower* set of openings — those farthest away from the mouthpiece. Unlike traditional re-corder pictures and diagrams, the illustration below is shown from the *player's* view rather than the observer's.

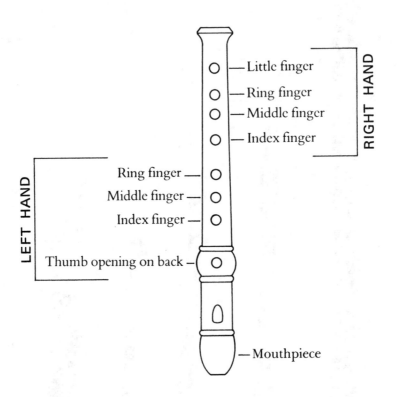

Playing

To produce the most desirable sound on the recorder, the player must blow gently and make certain that the openings are completely covered. Pressure on the openings should be with the cushion part of each finger — not the tip — and firm enough to leave a slight impression when the finger is lifted. Too strong a blow or any escape of air will result in a whistle or a squeak and assorted complaints from passersby.

Different combinations of fingerings produce different notes. Solid black circles on a recorder fingering chart indicate the openings that should be covered in order to produce the note specified.

To play, hold the recorder in the left hand with the thumb covering the opening on the underside. Cover the first opening of the upper group firmly with the left index finger. Form the word "too" and blow gently. The pitch will be B:

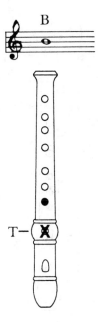

Cover the second opening of the same (upper) group with the left middle finger, keeping the index finger down also. The pitch will be A:

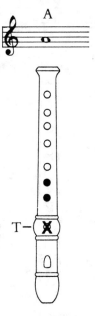

Keeping the index and middle fingers down, cover the third opening with the left ring finger. The pitch will be G:

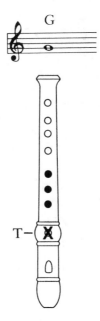

Note that the tune descends as the three fingers of the left hand also descend in turn.

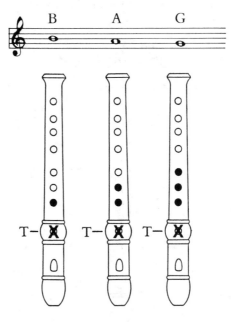

To play the reverse ascending progression (G A B) begin with the upper group of openings covered with three fingers of the left hand, then lifting each finger in turn beginning with the ring finger, followed by the middle, then the index:

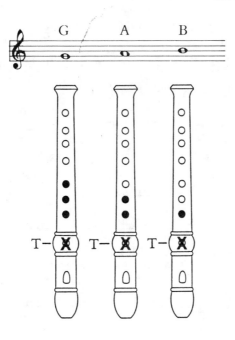

Practice Melodies

Fingering for the notes C (third space) and D (fourth line) are shown below.

For C, the middle finger of the left hand covers the second opening of the upper group, with the thumb covering the thumb opening on the underside. For D, simply remove the thumb, leaving the finger on the second opening.

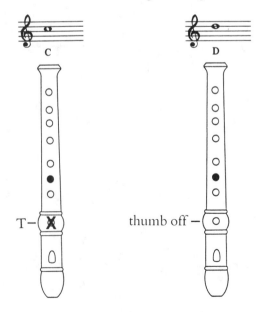

Practice Melodies

ODE TO JOY (excerpt)

BEETHOVEN

ANGELS WE HAVE HEARD ON HIGH (excerpt)

An - gels we have heard on high   sweet - ly sing - ing   o.'er the plains

And the moun - tains in re-ply   ech - o - ing their glad re - frain.

JINGLE BELLS

JAMES PIERPONT

More songs in the key of G may be played if the F♯ position is learned. As shown in the diagram below, F♯ (first space) is sounded by covering the thumb opening and all three openings of the upper group with the left hand and the second and third openings of the lower group with the middle and ring fingers of the right hand (index finger of right hand is not used for this note).

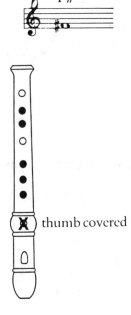

thumb covered

Practice Melodies (Note F♯ in Key Signature)

Melodies spanning an octave require D and E below F♯.

For E, cover all openings of the upper group with the left hand and the first *two* openings of the lower group with the right hand index and middle fingers (thumb opening covered):

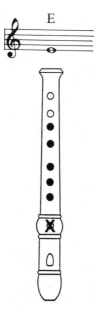

For D, cover all openings of the upper group with the left hand and the first *three* openings of the lower group with the right hand index, middle and ring fingers (thumb opening covered):

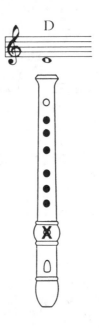

Practice Melodies *(Note F♯ in Key Signature)*

GOOD KING WENCESLAS

Traditional Carol

Allegretto

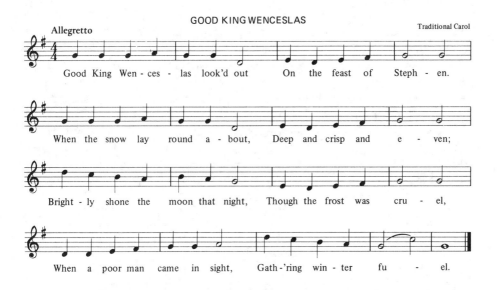

Good King Wen - ces - las look'd out   On the feast of Steph - en.

When the snow lay round a - bout,   Deep and crisp and e - ven;

Bright - ly shone the moon that night,   Though the frost was cru - el,

When a poor man came in sight,   Gath -'ring win - ter fu - el.

AURA LEE

W. W. Fosdick

George Poulton

BICYCLE BUILT FOR TWO

HARRY DACRE

Dai - sy, Dai - sy, give me your an - swer

true.___ I'm half cra - zy all for the

love of you.____ It won't be a styl - ish mar - riage;____ I can't af - ford a car - riage,____ But you'll look sweet up - on the seat of a bi - cy - cle built for two.____

GOOD NIGHT, LADIES

Good night, la - dies, good night, la - dies,
Good night, la - dies, We're going to leave you now.
Mer - ri - ly we roll a - long, roll a - long, roll a - long,
Mer - ri - ly we roll a - long, o'er the deep blue sea.

YANKEE DOODLE

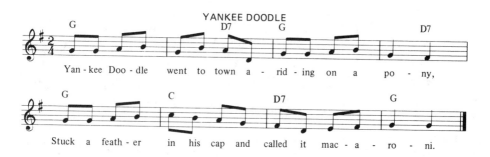

Yan - kee Doo - dle went to town a - rid - ing on a po - ny,
Stuck a feath - er in his cap and called it mac - a - ro - ni.

For additional practice see also Practice Melodies and song on p. 137 (under *Key of D*) and song on p. 138.

Sounding middle C requires extremely gentle blowing as well as firm, carefully complete covering of *all* openings.

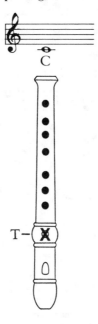

Practice Melodies

MORNING HAS BROKEN

THE WABASH CANNONBALL

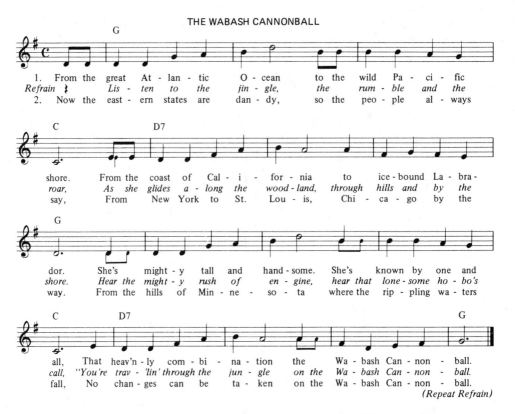

1. From the great At - lan - tic   O - cean   to the   wild   Pa - ci - fic
Refrain {   *Lis - ten   to   the   jin - gle,   the   rum - ble   and   the*
2. Now the east - ern states are   dan - dy,   so the   peo - ple   al - ways

shore.   From the   coast   of   Cal - i - for - nia   to   ice - bound La - bra -
roar,   As she   glides   a - long the   wood - land,   through   hills   and   by   the
say,   From   New York to   St.   Lou - is,   Chi - ca - go   by   the

dor.   She's   might - y   tall   and   hand - some.   She's   known   by   one   and
shore.   Hear the   might - y   rush   of   en - gine,   hear that   lone - some   ho - bo's
way.   From the   hills   of   Min - ne - so - ta   where the   rip - pling   wa - ters

all,   That   heav'n - ly   com - bi - na - tion   the   Wa - bash Can - non - ball.
call,   "You're   trav - 'lin' through the   jun - gle   on the   Wa - bash Can - non - ball.
fall,   No   chan - ges   can   be   ta - ken   on the   Wa - bash Can - non - ball.

(Repeat Refrain)

The generally accepted fingering for F is with all openings of the upper group (including the thumb) covered, and the first, third, and fourth openings of the lower group covered. Note that the middle finger of the right hand is not used, since the second opening of the lower group remains uncovered.

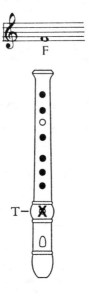

F

Practice Melodies

Depending upon the type of recorder used, some fingering charts may show the note F fingered as follows:

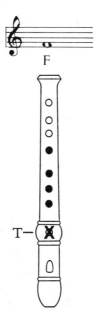

F

AULD LANG SYNE

ROBERT BURNS
Scotch Air

Should auld ac-quain-tance   be   for-got And   nev - er brought to   mind, Should

Refrain

auld   ac-quain-tance   be   for-got And   days of auld lang   syne?____ For

auld ___ lang ___ syne, my dear, For ___ auld ___ lang ___ syne; We'll
take   a   cup   of   kind - ness yet, For ___ auld ___ lang ___ syne.

ROW, ROW, ROW YOUR BOAT

Round

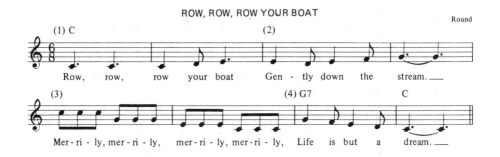

(1) C   (2)
Row,   row,   row   your boat   Gen - tly down   the   stream. ___

(3)   (4) G7   C
Mer - ri - ly, mer - ri - ly, mer - ri - ly, mer - ri - ly, Life is but   a   dream. ___

Play as a round.

ON TOP OF OLD SMOKEY

Southern Mountain Song

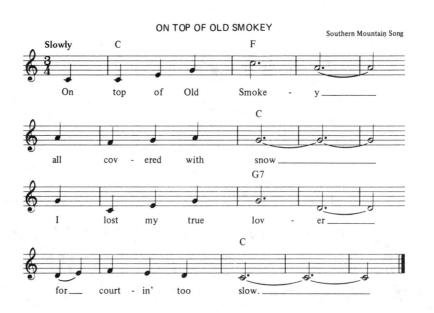

Slowly   C   F
On   top   of   Old   Smoke - y _____

                                        C
all   cov - ered   with   snow _____

                                        G7
I   lost   my   true   lov - er _____

                                        C
for ___ court - in' too   slow. _____

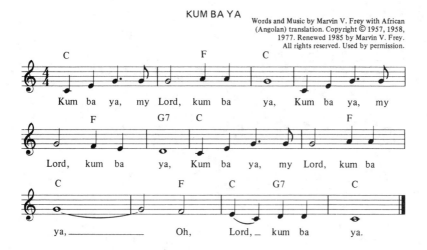

KUM BA YA

Playing songs in the key of F will require the frequent use of B flat (B♭), sounded by covering the first and third openings of the upper group with the index and ring fingers of the left hand respectively, and the first opening of the lower group with the index finger of the right hand (thumb opening covered).

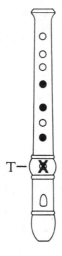

Practice Melodies (Note B♭ in Key Signature)

WE PRAISE THY NAME

English Words by CLARENCE WALWORTH
Traditional German Melody

1. Ho - ly   God,___ we   praise___ Thy   name.   Lord   of   all ___ we
2. Hark!   the   loud___   ce - les - tial   hymn   An - gel   choirs___ a -

bow___ be - fore Thee;   All   on   earth___ Thy   scep - ter ac - claim,
bove___ are   rais - ing!   Cher - u - bim___ and   ser - a - phim

All   in   Heav - en   a - bove___ a - dore Thee.   Bound - less   is   Thy
In   un - ceas - ing   cho - rus   prais - ing;   Fill   the   heav'ns with

vast   do - main.   Ev - er - last - ing   is___ Thy   reign.
sweet   ac - cord,   Ho - ly,   ho - ly,   ho - ly   Lord!

ALL THROUGH THE NIGHT

Traditional Welsh

F   B♭   G7   C   B♭   C7   F

HONEY, YOU CAN'T LOVE ONE

Traditional American Song

1. Hon - ey, you can't love one, ____

Hon - ey, you can't love one, ____

You can't love one and still have your fun,

Oh, Hon - ey, you can't love one. ____

For additional practice see also songs and Practice Melodies on pp. 25, 29, 135, and 136 ("Deaf Woman's Courtship").

Recorder Fingering Charts

In the complete recorder fingering charts shown below, note that some sharped and flatted notes are sounded by covering just half of an opening, indicated by half a black dot or by the symbol ½ next to the T for the thumb opening.

$\mathbb{X}$ = thumb opening covered

$\overset{\cdot\cdot}{(\,\,)}$ = thumb opening uncovered

Soprano Recorder Fingering Chart
English or Baroque

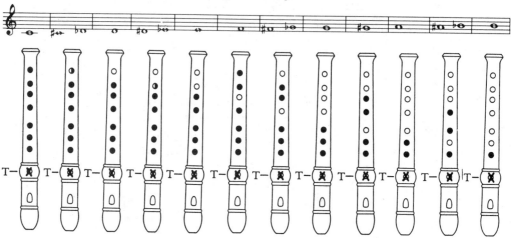

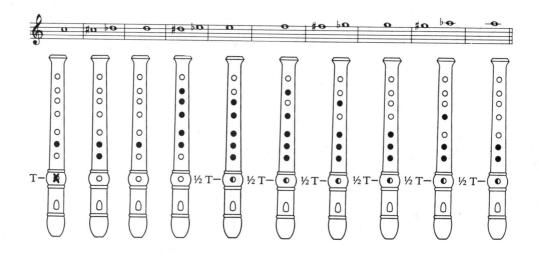

German fingering is very similar to the *English* or *Baroque* with the following exceptions:

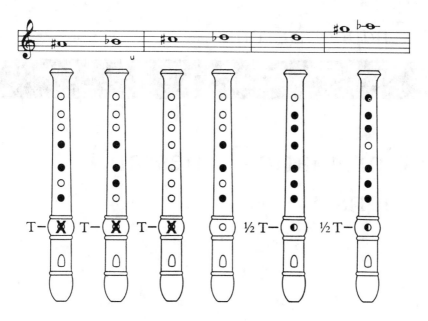

ACTIVITIES

1. Have one group sing the melody of a song while another group plays the chord roots on recorders (see "Creating Harmony," p. 215).

2. Use recorders in place of voice to sound the descants to songs shown on pp. 200, 202, and 220.

3. Create original descants to play with songs of choice (see "Creating Harmony," p. 215).

4. Substitute recorders for voices on one or all parts in selected rounds and part songs (see pp. 197, 198, and 226).

5. Combine with Autoharp, bells, piano, and rhythm instruments to play songs of choice.

Chapter Seven

Chromatic Tones and Signs

CHROMATIC TONES

Most of the melodies that have appeared thus far have been built on the tones of the major scale: DO RE MI FA SOL LA TI DO. Although an endless variety of tunes can flow from varied arrangements of these scale tones, there are other kinds of tones that may be used to add color and interest to melody. These are known as *chromatic tones*. Chromatic tones are scale tones that have been altered through the use of *chromatic signs*:

♯ *sharp*
♭ *flat*
♮ *natural* (also called *cancel*)

QUESTIONS

1. Two kinds of tones in music are scale tones and _____ tones.
2. _____ signs are used to alter scale tones.
3. This is an example of a chromatic sign: _____.

Answers p. 296

The sharps and flats found in the key signature of any piece of music are *not* chromatic tones for they *belong* to a given key and scale. Any note that is not native to a given key is considered a chromatic tone. In the example below, F♮ belongs to the key of G because it appears in the key signature; therefore, it is not a chromatic tone but a native one. A♮, however, does *not* appear in the key signature, thus A♮ must be considered a chromatic tone in this key:

scale tone chromatic tone

QUESTIONS

4. All the sharps and flats found in key signatures are chromatic tones. (True, False)

5. Chromatic tones are those tones that are _____ _____ to a given key.

Answers p. 296

Chromatic Signs

A chromatic tone occurring within the body of the song is easily identified because of the presence of one of the chromatic signs (♯, ♭, ♮). The chromatic sign must be placed directly in *front* of the note on the same line or space as the note it is to affect. When referring to the status of the note we say "G sharp," "B flat" (or whatever designation) even though the chromatic sign *precedes* the note when written on the staff.

chromatic tone   chromatic tone   chromatic tone

Whether the note affected by the chromatic sign is to be sounded a half step higher or a half step lower is dependent on two things:

1. the kind of chromatic sign used (♯, ♭, or ♮);
2. the status of the note in the key signature of the song.

When the note has been neither sharped nor flatted in the key signature:

a *sharp* (♯) beside the note signifies a chromatic tone a half step *higher*:

a *flat* (♭) beside the note signifies a chromatic tone a half step *lower*:

QUESTIONS

6. When a scale tone is neither sharped nor flatted in the key signature, a chromatic tone a half step higher is represented by a _____ (♯, ♭, ♮).

7. When a note is neither sharped nor flatted in the key signature, a flat (♭) placed beside the note indicates that the note is to be played or sung a half step _____ (higher, lower).

Answers p. 296

A *natural* (♮) beside the note could mean that the note is to be sounded either higher or lower, depending on the status of the note in the key signature. In the example shown below there is one flat—B—in the key signature. B♭ *belongs* in the key of F. It is the 4th tone (FA) of the scale in this key.

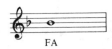

FA

The presence of the natural sign transforms B♭ the scale tone, into B♮ the *chromatic* tone—in this example, a chromatic tone a half step *higher* than B♭. To sound B♮ (B natural) on the keyboard, the white key B is played in place of the black key B♭:

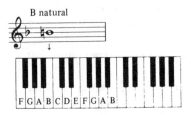

In the example shown below, C♯ belongs in the key of D. It is the 7th scale tone TI in this key:

The presence of the natural sign (♮) transforms C♯ the scale tone into C♮, the *chromatic* tone a half step *lower* than C♯. To sound C♮ (C natural) on the keyboard the white key C is played in place of the black key C♯:

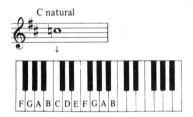

QUESTIONS

8. A chromatic tone a half step above B♭ would be played on a _____ (black, white) key.

9. To represent a chromatic tone a half step below C♯, a (♯, ♭, ♮) _____would be used.

10. A chromatic tone a half step below C♯ is called C _____ (flat, natural).

Answers p. 296

Chromatic Scale

A *chromatic scale* is made up entirely of half steps and may be played from any note on the keyboard. There is a common misconception that all the black keys on the keyboard are chromatic tones. The fact is that the key of C is the only key in which all the chromatic tones fall on the black keys, as shown in the example below beginning on C:

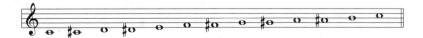

When executing a chromatic scale beginning on any note other than C, chromatic tones may fall on white keys as well.

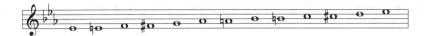

┌─ **QUESTIONS** ─────────────────────────────────

11. A chromatic scale is made up of whole steps and half steps. (True, False)
12. Chromatic tones are always played on the black keys. (True, False)
13. In the key of C, chromatic tones always fall on the black keys. (True, False)
14. A chromatic scale may be played from any note on the keyboard. (True, False)

Answers p. 296

└───

Singing Chromatic Tone Syllables a Half Step Higher

When singing with syllables, chromatic tones bear special names that are derived from the scale tones. For chromatic tones a half step higher, the first letter of the syllable name is used, with the sound of "ee"—spelled *i*—added. For example, the first letter of LA, the *scale* tone, with an *i* added, becomes LI ("lee"), the chromatic tone. A chromatic tone a half step above SOL would be SI ("see").

When singing an ascending chromatic scale, the syllable names for chromatic tones a half step higher are used:

DO *DI* RE *RI* MI FA *FI* SOL *SI* LA *LI* TI DO

┌─ **QUESTIONS** ─────────────────────────────────

15. A chromatic tone a half step above DO would be called
    _____.

16. A chromatic tone a half above RE would be called _____.

17. Chromatic tones a half step higher are derived from the first _____ of the scale tone with the sound of _____ added.

Answers p. 296

└───

A chromatic sign in front of a note affects that note for the remainder of the measure:

If the chromatic sign used is a sharp (♯), then a natural or cancel will return the note to its original form within the same measure:

If the chromatic sign used is a cancel, then a flat will return the note to its original form within the same measure.

A measure bar erases the effect of any chromatic sign used in the previous measure:

QUESTIONS

18. A chromatic sign in front of a note affects that note for the remainder of the measure. (True, False)

19. The effect of any chromatic sign is carried over from measure to measure in any given piece of music. (True, False)

20. A measure bar erases the effect of any chromatic sign in the previous measure. (True, False)

21. When a sharp has been used to represent a chromatic tone a half step higher, then a _____ will return the note to its original form within the same measure. When a cancel or natural has been used to represent a chromatic tone a half step higher, then a _____ will return the note to its original form within the same measure.

Answers p. 296

Practice Melodies for Chromatics a Half Step Higher (See NOTE p. 19)

Singing Chromatic Tone Syllables a Half Step Lower

The syllable names for chromatic tones a half step lower than the scale tone are also derived from the scale tone names by using the first letter of the syllable name and adding the sound of "ay"—spelled *e*. For example, the chromatic tone a half step below LA would be LE ("lay"). A chromatic tone a half step below TI would be TE ("tay"). Since RE already has the "ay" sound, it becomes RAH.

When singing a descending chromatic scale, the syllable names for chromatic tones a half step lower are used:

DO TI *TE* LA *LE* SOL *SE* FA MI *ME* RE *RAH* DO

QUESTIONS

22. A chromatic tone a half step below MI is called _____.
23. A chromatic tone a half step below RE is called _____.
24. TE is the chromatic tone a half step below _____.

Answers p. 296

A chromatic sign in front of a note affects that note for the remainder of the measure:

LA LE   LE

If the chromatic sign used is a flat (♭), then a natural or cancel will return the note to its original form within the same measure:

LA LE   LA

(Returning a note to its "original form" simply means erasing the effect of the chromatic sign by replacing what the chromatic sign removed.) If the chromatic sign used is a cancel (♮), then a sharp will return the note to its original form within the same measure:

TI TE

TI   TE   TI

A measure bar cancels the effect of any chromatic sign used in the previous measure:

TI TE   TI

QUESTIONS

25. When a flat has been used to represent a chromatic tone a half step lower, then a _____ will return the note to its original form within the same measure.

26. When a cancel or natural has been used to represent a chromatic tone a half step lower, then a _____ will return the note to its original form within the same measure.

Answers p. 296

Practice Melodies for Chromatics a Half Step Lower (See NOTE p. 19)

CHROMATIC SUMMARY

Chromatic Tones a Half Step Higher (Read *up*)	Scale Tone	Chromatic Tones a Half Step Lower (Read *down*)
	DO	
	TI	
li ←	LA	→ te
si ←	SOL	→ le
fi ←	FA	→ se
	MI	
ri ←	RE	→ me
di ←	DO	→ rah

The Double Sharp (×)

Double sharps (and double flats) are found more frequently in instrumental music, but occasionally they do occur in a vocal score.

When a scale tone has been sharped in the key signature, a double sharp is used to represent a chromatic tone a half step above the scale tone. In the example below, F (SOL) has been sharped in the key signature, thus a double sharp is required for the chromatic tone SI a half step above SOL:

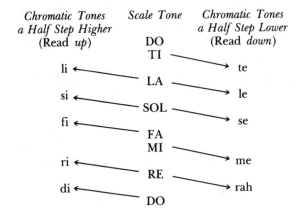

DO   SOL LA SI   LA

When played on an instrument, obviously F double sharped will be the note G; however, it is still written as shown above.

To return the double sharped note to its original form within the measure, a cancel and a sharp are used:

DO   SOL LA SI LA SOL

As stated previously, measure bars cancel the effect of any chromatic sign and would produce the same result as the cancel and the sharp.

The Double Flat (♭♭)

When a scale tone has been flatted in the key signature, a *double flat* is used to represent a chromatic tone a half step below the scale tone. In the example below, B (LA) has been flatted in the key signature; thus a double flat (♭♭) is required for the chromatic tone a half step below (LE):

LA   LE

When playing an instrument a double flatted B would obviously be the note A; however, it is written as shown above.

To return the note to its original form within the measure, a cancel and a flat are used.

LE   LA

QUESTIONS

27. This sign ♭♭ is a _____ _____.
28. A double sharp must be used to represent a chromatic tone a half step higher when the scale tone has been _____ in the key signature.

Answers p. 296

Identify the chromatic tones in the songs that follow.

YOU'RE A GRAND OLD FLAG

GEORGE M. COHAN

You're a grand old flag, you're a high-fly-ing flag; And for-ev-er, in peace may you wave;___ ___ You're the em-blem of the land I love, The home of the free and the brave.___ ___ Ev-'ry heart beats true, un-der Red, White and Blue; Where there's nev-er a boast or brag;___ ___ But, should auld ac-quain-tance be for-got, Keep your eye on the grand old flag.___

GOD'S GONNA SET THIS WORLD ON FIRE

Spiritual

God's gon-na set this world on fi-re

God's gon-na set this world on fi - re one of these days, Hal - le - lu - jah!

God's gon-na set this world on fi - re God's gon - na

set this world on fi - re one of these days.

ALL ROUND THE MOUNTAIN

American Folk Song
Collected by Marshall Bartholomew

All round the moun-tain, charm-ing Bet - sy, _____ All round the

moun-tain, Lau - ra Lee,_____ If I nev - er

see her no more, May the good Lord re - mem - ber me._____

1. Town gal, _____ she rides a car - riage, _____ Coun-try gal, _____
2. Town gal, _____ she wears a sat - in dress, _____ Coun-try gal, _____
3. Town gal, _____ she wears high - heel shoes, _____ Coun-try gal, _____

_____ she rides the same,_____ Moun - tain gal rides an
_____ she wears the same,_____ Moun - tain gal wears a
_____ she wears the same,_____ Moun - tain gal wears

old ox - cart, _____ But she gets there just the same._____
cal - i - co dress,_____
no shoes at all, _____

DOWN BY THE RIVERSIDE

Spiritual

1. I'm gon-na lay down my sword and shield, down by the riv-er-side, down by the riv-er-side, down by the riv-er-side, Gon-na lay down my sword and shield, down by the riv-er-side, Gon-na stud-y___ war no more.___

Chorus

I ain't gon-na stud-y war no more, I ain't gon-na stud-y war no more. I ain't gon-na stud-y___ war no more.___ more, I ain't gon-na stud-y___ war no more.___

CONSIDER YOURSELF

From the Columbia Pictures-Romulus Film
OLIVER! Words and Music by Lionel Bart
© Copyright 1960 Lakeview Music Co., Ltd.,
London, England
TRO-Hollis Music, Inc., New York controls
all publication rights for the U.S. and Canada.
Used by permission.

Moderate march tempo

Con - sid - er your-self ___ at home, ___ Con -

sid - er your - self _____ one of the fam - i - ly. _____ I've

tak - en to you _____ so strong, _____ It's

clear we're go - ing to get a - long! Con -

sid - er your - self _____ well in, _____ Con -

sid - er your - self _____ part of the fur - ni - ture. _____ There

is - n't a lot _____ to spare; _____ Who

cares? What - ev - er we've got we share! { If it should
{ No - bod - y

chance to be, we should see some hard - er days, _____ Emp - ty
tries to be, lah - di - dah and up - pit - y, _____ There's a

lard - er days, _____ why grouse? _____ Al - ways a
cup 'o tea _____ for all. _____ On - ly it's

chance we'll meet some - bod - y to foot the bill, _____ Then the
wise, to be hand - y with a roll - ing pin, _____ When the

drinks are on the house! _____ }
land - lord comes to call! _____ } Con -

sid - er your - self _____ our mate, _____ We

don't want to have _____ no fuss, _____ For

af - ter some con - sid - er - a - tion, we can state: Con -

sid - er your - self _____ one of us.

PUT YOUR HAND IN THE HAND

Words and Music by GENE MacLELLAN
© 1970 by BEECHWOOD MUSIC OF CANADA.
U.S. rights assigned to and controlled by
BEECHWOOD MUSIC CORP. Used by permission.
International Copyright Secured.
All Rights Reserved

Put your hand in the hand of the man who stilled _ the

wa - ters, _____ Put your hand in the hand of the

man who calmed _ the sea. Take a look at your-self and - a

you can look at oth - ers dif-f'rent - ly _____ By put-tin' your

hand in the hand of the man from - a Gal - i - lee. _____

BILL BAILEY

Words and Music by Hughie Cannon

Won't you come home, Bill Bai - ley, Won't you come home,

She cried the whole night long? _____

I'll do the dish - es, hon - ey, I'll pay the rent.

I know I done you wrong. _____

'Mem - ber that rain - y eve - ning I drove you out With

noth - in' but a fine - tooth comb? _____ I

know I'm to blame, Well, ___ ain't that a shame, Bill

Bai - ley, won't you please come home?

Chapter Eight

Major, Minor, and Other Modes

A scale is sometimes referred to as a *mode*. The most frequently used modes in music are the *major* and the *minor*. The term *major* refers to a prescribed arrangement of eight scale tones (beginning and ending on DO) in whole and half step intervals (see p. 103). Different interval arrangements produce different modes. In the major mode the keynote or tonal center is DO. In the minor mode the keynote or tonal center is LA. Songs in the minor mode frequently end on the syllable LA (see songs on pp. 181, 182, and 183).

QUESTIONS

1. Two of the most common modes in music are _____ and _____.
2. Major scales begin and end on the syllable _____.
3. Different interval arrangements produce different _____.
4. Minor songs usually end on the syllable _____.
5. DO is the keynote or tonal center of the _____ mode.

Answers p. 296

MINOR SCALES

Just as music in the major mode is based on the major scale, so music in the minor mode is based on the *minor scale*. A major scale begins and ends on DO, a minor scale begins and ends on LA. Because of the different starting tone, the whole and half step intervals in the minor scale will fall in different places from those of the major scale. This is what produces the effect of the "minor" sound. Note examples of each below:

QUESTIONS

6. Minor scales begin and end on the syllable _____.
7. In a minor scale LA is the number _____.
8. The interval pattern in a minor scale is (the same as, different from) that of a major scale.

Answers p. 297

Forms of Minor Scales

Minor scales come in assorted forms, adding to the interest of music based on them. The simplest form of minor scale is the *natural* (sometimes called *pure* or *normal*) *minor* containing the tones LA TI DO RE MI FA SOL LA in that order ascending and in reverse order descending: (note half steps between 2–3 and 5–6):

The *harmonic minor* form is easily identified by the presence of a sharp (♯) or natural (♮) appearing beside the seventh tone of the scale (SOL), indicating that it is to be sounded a half step higher. When singing the harmonic minor scale with syllables, SOL is called SI. Tones of the harmonic minor scale are LA TI DO RE MI FA SI LA in that order ascending and in reverse order descending:

The sounding of SOL a half step higher also increases the size of the interval between the 6th and 7th tones of the harmonic minor scale to 1½ steps:

In the *melodic minor* scale the tones FA and SOL are sounded a half step higher — becoming FI and SI respectively — in the ascending form, but revert back to FA and SOL again in the descending form. Thus the descending melodic minor scale is the same as the descending *natural* minor scale:

Identification of specific minor forms in given musical selections may be made by simply checking the presence of a natural or sharp sign placed before the 6th and 7th tones (FA and SOL). If only the 7th tone is affected, the song may be assumed to be in the *harmonic* minor form. If both the 6th and 7th tones are affected, then the melodic minor form is indicated. The absence of any such signs before the 6th or 7th tones would strongly indicate that the song is in the natural minor form.

QUESTIONS

9. There are _____ forms of minor scales.
10. The _____ minor form sounds different descending than it does ascending.

11. In the _____ minor form the 7th tone (SOL) is sung or played a half step higher ascending and descending.

12. These tones: LA TI DO RE MI FA SOL LA are the tones of the _____ minor form.

Answers p. 297

The songs that follow represent various forms of the minor. Try to identify each.

THE WRAGGLE-TAGGLE GYPSIES

Old English Ballad

1. There__ were three gyp - sies a - come to my door, And
2. Then__ she pulled off her __ silk - fin -ish'd gown And
3. It was late last night when my lord came home, In

down - stairs ran this - a la - dy, O! The one sang high and an -
put on hose of leath - er, O! The rag - ged rags a -
quir - ing for his la - dy, O! The ser - vants said on

oth - er sang low, And the oth - er sang "Bon-ny, bon-ny Bis - cay, O!"
bout our door, And she's gone__with the wrag-gle - tag - gle gyp - sies, O!
ev - 'ry hand, 7 "She's gone__with the wrag-gle - tag - gle gyp - sies, O!"

HALLELUJAH

Folk Song from Israel
From THE GOOD TIMES SONGBOOK by
James Leisy
© 1974 by James Leisy Music
Used by permission of the publisher,
Abingdon Press.

Hal - le - lu - jah hal - le - lu - jah hal - le - lu - jah hal - le - lu

Hal - le - lu - jah hal - le - lu - jah hal - le - lu - jah hal - le - lu

Hal - le - lu - jah hal - le - lu hal - le - lu - jah hal - le - lu

The minor song "For Thy Gracious Blessing," shown below, may be sung as a canon with the second voice entering when the first voice begins the second measure, as shown by the numbers 1 and 2. (See *Canon* p. 198.)

Note: The first eight measures of "Joshua Fit the Battle of Jericho," shown below, may be sung as a partner song with the first eight measures of "Go Down Moses" (p. 183). (See "Partner Songs," p. 195.)

D.C. al Fine

Josh - u - a   in the bat - tle of   Jer - i - cho.

GO DOWN MOSES

Spiritual

When   Is - rael   was   in   E - gypt's   land   Let my   peo - ple

go   Op - pressed   so   hard   they   could   not   stand   Let my   peo - ple

go   Go down,   Mo - ses,   'Way   down   in   E - gypt   land ___

Tell ___   old   Phar - aoh, ___   Let my   peo - ple   go.

SHALOM ALEHEM

Jewish Folk Song

Hĕ - vĕ - nu   sha - lom   a - lĕ - hem,   Hĕ - vĕ - nu

sha - lom   a - lĕ - hem,   Hĕ - vĕ - nu   sha - lom   a -

lĕ - hem,   Hĕ - vĕ - nu   sha - lom,   sha - lom,   sha - lom   a - lĕ - hem.

See pages 197, 218, 225, and 229 for additional songs in minor.

Transposing the chord letters to the key of F may be done either by (1) determining the number of each chord (I, IV, etc.) according to the key signature, then matching the letter name in the new key to the chord number or (2) by counting letters alphabetically. For example, in the new key of F, F is four letters above C; thus every C chord becomes F, every F chord shown in the given song becomes B♭, and every G7 chord becomes C7 in the new key.

QUESTIONS

41. Transpose the chord letter names shown in Example *a.* to chord letter names suitable for the key shown in Example *b.*

Ex. a

Ex. b

42. Insert the numerals from Example *c.* below in the same succession under the staff in Example *d.*, then translate into appropriate letter names (write in above staff) according to the new key shown.

Ex. c

Ex. d

Answers p. 298

Relative Minor Keys

Every major key has what is known as its *relative* minor. The common bond between them is the key signature. For example, the signature of one sharp for the key of G major is the same as that for the relative key of *e minor*:

Key of G major   Key of e minor

The relative minor of any given major key may be found by simply counting down from the keynote DO of the major key to the keynote LA of the minor key—an interval of 1½ steps:

The name of the line or space upon which LA falls is the name of the relative minor key.

In the key of F major shown below DO is on F:

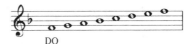

DO

The relative minor of F major is found by counting down from the keynote DO (F) an interval of 1½ steps to LA:

LA is on D, thus the relative minor of F major is d minor. (Minor keys are usually written in lower-case letters.)

QUESTIONS

13. The relative minor of the major key of F is _____.
14. The common bond between each major scale and its relative minor is the _____ _____.
15. The relative minor of any major key is determined by counting down an interval of _____ steps from the major keynote DO.

Answers p. 297

When counting down the 1½ step interval from DO to LA, it is important to note whether the line or space upon which LA falls has been flatted or sharped in the given major key signature. If it has, then the word "sharp" or "flat" must be added to the letter name of the minor key. In the example shown below, LA falls on the third space C which has a sharp on it in the key signature; thus the name of the relative minor of this key (E major) would be C♯ minor:

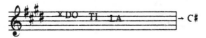

In connection with the foregoing, it should be noted that when counting the 1½ step intervals from DO to LA, all sharps and flats that occur within the 1½ steps must be counted in.

QUESTIONS

16. In the major keys shown below, count down from DO to LA (1½ steps) to find the relative minor of each major key. Insert LA in its proper place on the staff provided and name the relative minor keys:

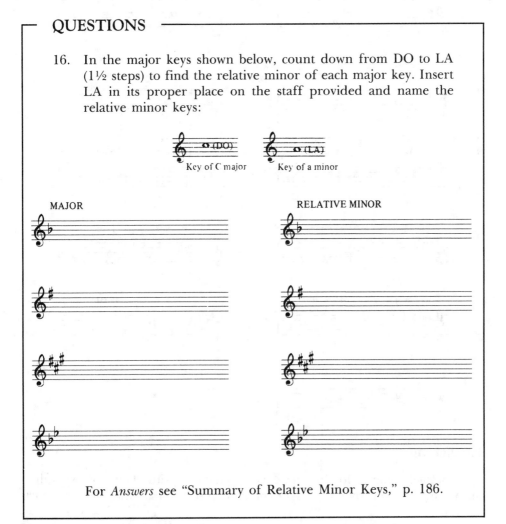

For *Answers* see "Summary of Relative Minor Keys," p. 186.

SUMMARY OF RELATIVE MINOR KEYS

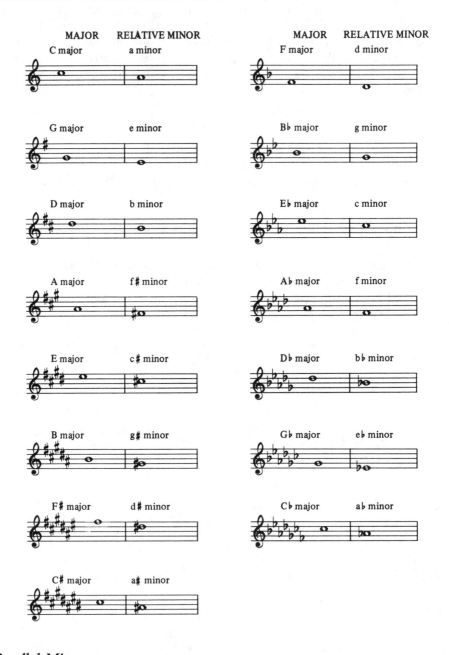

Parallel Minor

Parallel minors do not share key signatures with their corresponding major keys. Rather, they represent companion scales that have the same starting tone:

C Major scale

Parallel Minor Scale—c minor

G Major Scale

Parallel Minor Scale—g minor

QUESTIONS

17. *Relative* minor keys are related to major keys through their
    _____ _____.

18. A *parallel* minor key has the same _____ _____
    as the given major key.

19. Parallel minor keys do not have the same _____
    _____ as their major key companions.

Answers p. 297

The song below is shown first in the major key, then in the minor. Note that they share the same starting tone but have different key signatures. Play the major tune first on the piano or bells, then the minor, observing the flats indicated.

TWINKLE TWINKLE

Key of c minor

Early Modes

A further source of other scales or *modes* is early church music. As shown below, each mode begins on a different tone; thus the arrangement of whole and half steps differs with the mode. Note that the Ionian is an old friend, the C major scale, while the Aeolian is its relative—a minor. These two modes came into the greatest use over the centuries. Recently, however, many songwriters have used some of the other early modes in their contemporary tunes.

Play each of the following modes on a keyboard instrument (note that they are all played on the white keys). For additional ACTIVITIES, see p. 194.

EARLY MODES

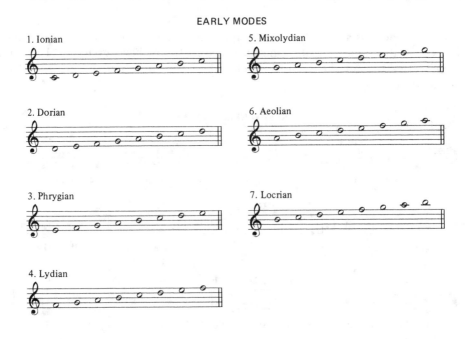

1. Ionian

2. Dorian

3. Phrygian

4. Lydian

5. Mixolydian

6. Aeolian

7. Locrian

Can you identify the modes of the songs that follow?

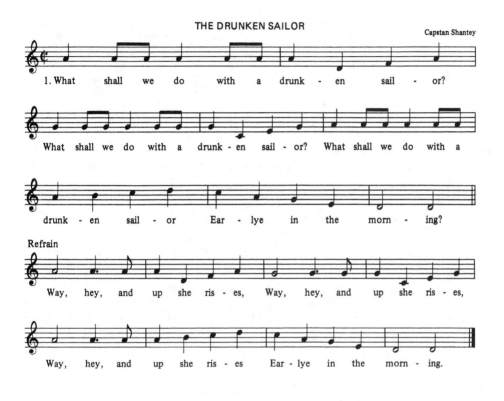

MORE SCALES AND MODES

Pentatonic

The *pentatonic scale* is considered "universal" because it is found in so much of the folk and traditional music of the world. It is a five-tone scale with no half steps, consisting of the tones DO RE MI SOL LA:

A pentatonic scale may be sung or played from any DO; however, beginning on the black key F♯ and playing all the succeeding black keys in order is an easy way of sounding it:

See ACTIVITIES, p. 194.

Many traditional American folk songs as well as spirituals and hymns are based on tones of the pentatonic scale. These include "Swing Low, Sweet Chariot" (p. 196), "Riddle Song" (p. 30), and "Amazing Grace" (shown below).

AMAZING GRACE

Words by JOHN NEWTON
Early American Melody

2. Twas grace that taught my heart to fear,
And grace my fears relieved;
How precious did that grace appear
The hour I first believed!

3. Through many dangers, toils and snares,
I have already come;
'Tis grace has brought me safe thus far,
And grace will lead me home.

The songs listed below are all built on tones of the pentatonic scale, and may be played on any keyboard instrument using only the black keys. Exploring tunes by ear on the black keys is an interesting experiment. Starting tones are given:

SONG	STARTING TONE
Auld Lang Syne	C♯
Goodbye Old Paint	D♯
Merrily We Roll Along	A♯
Old MacDonald	F♯

See ACTIVITIES p. 194.

Whole Tone Scale

Although the nineteenth-century French composer Claude Debussy did not originate the *whole tone* scale, he was a master in its use. Unlike many other composers who sought to tell a story through music, Debussy chose rather to evoke a mood. To many listeners the mood is frequently one of enchantment (See ACTIVITIES, p. 194.)

Blues Scale

The *blues scale*, like blues songs, is characterized by the lowered 3rd and 7th tones:

It has been suggested that these lowered tones evolved from the "bent" tones of the field hollers and calls among slaves in early America. Traditionally, the blues song is a twelve-bar (measure), three-phrase form, the words of which frequently express trouble in heart and mind. The words of each of the first two phrases are usually the same; the third phrase is different:

JOE TURNER BLUES

American Blues

As the singer completes the words of each phrase, the instrumentalists "improvise" briefly on the melody for a measure or two. Blues is considered to be one of the stages in the evolution of jazz, which in itself is characterized by improvisation.

Not all songs containing *blue* notes are classed as *blues*. Many of the folk melodies from the Appalachian Mountains frequently contain lowered 3rds and 7ths, sometimes even a lowered 6th as in the song "He's Gone Away," producing a plaintive effect.

In contrast to the plaintive sound of "He's Gone Away," note the upbeat feeling generated by the same lowered tones combined with a syncopated rhythm in the contemporary composed song "I'm Gonna Walk."

I'M GONNA WALK

Words and Music by DAVID EDDLEMAN

Walk with   me, ___   Walk with ___   me.

ACTIVITIES

1. Create original scales by varying traditional arrangements of whole and half steps.

2. Create original short melodies based on scales other than the major: pentatonic, whole tone, blues, etc.

3. Create a song in the blues form using the tones of the blues scale.

4. Explore the pentatonic scale using the black keys only on a keyboard instrument (bells, piano, etc.), then improvise a descant (see *descant* p. 199) or ostinato (see *ostinato* p. 218) using only the black keys. Create a second melody on the black keys to play against the descant or ostinato.

5. Set a favorite piece of haiku poetry to tones of the pentatonic scale.

6. Select a favorite short poem or create one, then set it to music based on the tones of any scale desired.

7. Change the song below ("Are You Sleeping?") from its major key to the relative minor key by altering the key signature, then play.

8. See also ACTIVITIES for resonator bells, p. 139–140.

ARE YOU SLEEPING   Round

Are   you   sleep - ing,   Are   you   sleep - ing
Frè - re   Jac - ques,   Frè - re   Jac - ques,

Broth - er   John,   Broth - er   John?
Dor - mez   vous,   Dor - mez   vous?

Morn - ing   bells   are   ring - ing,   Morn - ing   bells   are   ring - ing,
Son - nez   les   ma - ti - nes,   Son - nez   les   ma - ti - nes,

Ding   dang,   dong!   Ding,   dang,   dong!
Din,   dan,   don!   Din,   dan,   don!

Chapter Nine

███████████████████████████████████████

Harmony

Harmony results from the sounding together of two or more selected musical tones. It may be produced either vocally or instrumentally.

The presence or absence of harmony in a piece of music, as well as the arrangement of its other musical components, may determine the nature of its musical *texture*. For example, when a single line of melody is played or sung without any accompaniment, the texture is referred to as *monophonic*. A melody supported by vocal or instrumental chordal accompaniment produces *homophonic* texture. *Polyphonic* texture results from the simultaneous sounding of two or more independent melodies, and may be heard in various musical forms, from simple rounds to more involved fugues. Polyphonic music is also referred to as *contrapuntal* music.

A single large musical work, conceivably, may contain several different textures, ranging from thin to dense, depending on the desires of the composer and/or arranger.

HARMONIC DEVICES

As a beginning experience, "instant" harmony may be produced through such simple devices as partner songs, rounds, and descants.

Partner Songs

Partner songs are defined as songs that are harmonically compatible when sung simultaneously, such as "When the Saints Go Marching In" and "Swing Low Sweet Chariot," both shown below.

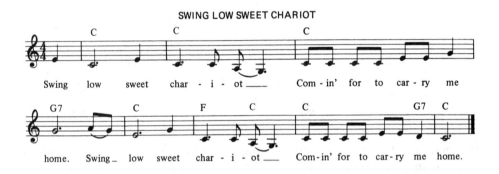

"Swing Low Sweet Chariot" may also be sung as a partner song with "Good Night, Ladies" and "Comin' Round the Mountain." "When the Saints Go Marching In" works well as a partner song with "This Train."

Examples of other songs that can be sung in partnership include:

*"Rock-a My Soul" and *"He's Got the Whole World in His Hands"
"Aloha Oe" (chorus only) and "This Land Is Your Land"
"My Bonnie" (chorus only) and "Man on the Flying Trapeze"
*"Are You Sleeping" and "Three Blind Mice" and *"Row Row Row Your Boat"
*"Go Tell Aunt Rhody" and *"Merrily We Roll Along"
*"Down the River" and *"Vive L'Amour" (choruses only)
*"Hey, Ho! Nobody Home" and *"Shalom, Chaverim"
*"Joshua Fit the Battle of Jericho" and *"Go Down Moses" (first eight measures only of both songs)

*Indicates songs found in this book. Since partner songs must be pitched in the same key, some songs shown may require transposing to compatible keys. (See "Transposition," p. 129.)

Rounds

Rounds are an imitative form in which each voice repeats the same melody but enters and departs at different times. Rounds may be in as few as two parts and as many as eight or more. In the rounds that follow, the numbers over the measure indicate where each part should enter.

HEY, HO! NOBODY HOME

Traditional English round

Hey, ho! No - bod - y home, Meat nor drink nor mon - ey have I none,

Yet I will be hap - py, — Hey, ho! No - bod - y home.

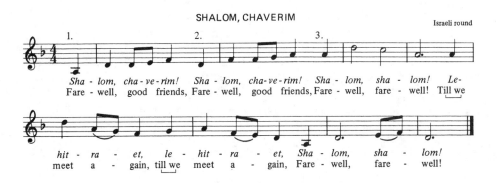

SHALOM, CHAVERIM

Israeli round

Sha - lom, cha - ve - rim! Sha - lom, cha - ve - rim! Sha - lom, sha - lom! Le-
Fare - well, good friends, Fare - well, good friends, Fare - well, fare - well! Till we

hit - ra - et, le - hit - ra - et, Sha - lom, sha - lom!
meet a - gain, till we meet a - gain, Fare - well, fare - well!

DONA NOBIS PACEM

Three-part round

Do-na no-bis pa - cem, pa-cem, do - na no - bis pa - cem.

Do - na no - bis pa-cem, do na no - bis pa - cem.

Do - na no - bis — pa-cem; do na no - bis pa - cem.

MUSIC ALONE SHALL LIVE

Canon

A *canon* is similar to a round in that the first voice is imitated by succeeding voices; however, unlike the round, the voices in a canon frequently
are arranged to end together, as shown below in "All Creatures of Our God
and King."

ALL CREATURES OF OUR GOD AND KING

Words From St. FRANCIS Of ASSISI
17th Century German Melody
English translation by WILLIAM H. DRAPER.
Used by arrangement with G. Schirmer, Inc.

burn - ing sun with gold - en beam, Thou sil - ver moon with soft - er

beam, Thou sil - ver moon with soft - er gleam! Al - le -

gleam! Al - le - lu - ia! Al - le - lu - ia! Al - le -

lu - ia! Al - le - lu - ia! Al - le - lu - ia! Al - le -

lu - ia! Al - le - lu - ia! Al - le - lu - ia!

TALLIS' CANON

Words by THOMAS KEN
Music by THOMAS TALLIS

Glo - ry to Thee, my God, this night, For

all the bless - ings of the light; Keep me, oh keep me,

King of kings, Be - neath Thine own al - might - y wings.

Descant

A *descant* (sometimes called a "countermelody") is a melody that may be played, sung, whistled, or hummed against the main melody of a song in order to produce harmony. Descants or countermelodies may range from simple chantlike tunes to those that are melodic enough to be complete melodies in themselves.

The descant for "Streets of Laredo" uses only three notes of the scale: MI, FA, and SOL. These may be whistled, hummed, sung on "oo" or "ah" or played on bells or recorder (see pp. 138 and 140).

STREETS OF LAREDO

Cowboy Song

1. As I walked out on the streets of La - re - do, As
2. "I see by your out - fit that you are a cow - boy," These

I ____ walked out in La - re - do one day, I
words he did say as I bold - ly walked by; "Come

spied a young cow - boy all wrapped in white lin - en, All
sit down be - side me and hear my sad sto - ry, I'm

wrapped in white lin - en and cold as the clay.
shot in the chest and I know I must die."

The following descant may also be played or sung with "Streets of Laredo."

STREETS OF LAREDO

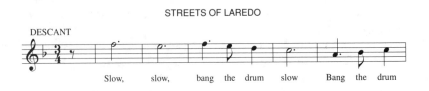

Slow, slow, bang the drum slow   Bang the drum

slow Bang the drum slow Low, low, play the fife

low Play the fife low, Oh, so low.

The "Boom-dee-ah-da" portion of "I Love the Mountains" may be used as a descant with the melody; the entire song may also be sung as a round.

I LOVE THE MOUNTAINS

I love the moun-tains, I love the roll-ing hills, I love the flow-ers,

I love the daf-fo-dils; I love the fire-side when all the lights are low.

Boom - dee - ah - da, Boom - dee - ah - da, Boom - dee - ah - da, Boom - dee - ah - da.

The descant for "Brother James' Air" shown below is an example of the more tuneful type:

BROTHER JAMES' AIR

Words by JAMES L. BAIN
Scottish Hymn Tune

Smoothly, reverently

1. The Lord's my shep - herd, I'll not want, He makes me down to lie In
2. My soul He doth re - store a - gain and me to walk doth make With -

pas - tures green, He lead - eth me the qui - et wa - ters by; He
in the paths of bless - ed - ness e'en for His own name's sake; With -

lead - eth me, He lead - eth me the qui - et wa - ters by.
in the paths of bless - ed - ness e'en for His own name's sake.

Descant for "BROTHER JAMES' AIR"

The descants and countermelodies shown below may be played or sung with songs found elsewhere in the book as indicated.

Descant for "WHEN THE SAINTS GO MARCHING IN"

When the saints,   march-ing in,   Saints go march-ing   in,

("Ah" or "Oo" _____)   Saints   go   march - ing   in.

Countermelody for "Pallet on the Floor (p. 62)

COUNTERMELODY (REFRAIN)

You   made   me   a   pal - let   on   the   floor.

Made me   a   pal - let on the floor.   Had no place to go, ___   you

o- pened up your door, ___   And you   made me a pal-let on ___ the   floor.

Countermelody for "Paddy Works on the Railway" (refrain only), p. 72.

COUNTERMELODY (REFRAIN)

Fil - li-mee - oo - ree - oo - ree - ay,   Fil - li-mee - oo - ree - oo - ree - ay,

Fil - li - mee - oo - ree - oo - ree - ay,   Oo - ree - ay. ___

ACTIVITIES

1. On a round or canon of choice, use different instruments (bells, recorder, voice, piano, etc.) and/or body movement for each voice as it enters (see pp. 197, 199).
2. Sing "Twinkle, Twinkle" as a canon (p. 187). Second voice enters as first voice completes the first measure.
3. Create a visual representation of a round or canon showing entrance of each voice at spaced intervals and imitation of the melody.
4. Create some original descants to selected tunes (see "Descants," p. 219).

The secret of the harmonious sounds produced in the performance of partner songs, rounds, and descants is revealed upon examination of how harmony is made.

CHORD STRUCTURE

A *chord* is a group of tones sounded simultaneously to produce harmony. A three-tone chord is sometimes called a *triad*. It is possible to build a triad or chord on any note of the scale in any key:

QUESTIONS

1. When two or more selected musical tones are sounded at the same time they produce the musical element known as

   _____.

2. When a chord contains only three tones it is sometimes called a _____.

Answers p. 297

The scale tone upon which each chord is built is known as the *root* of the chord. When constructing a chord, the root is counted as *one*. Three letters up the musical alphabet from the root is the third of the chord and five letters up the musical alphabet from the root is the fifth of the chord. Each chord contains a *root*, a *third*, and a *fifth*:

The musical interval between the *root* and the *third* of any major chord is two whole steps. The interval between the third and fifth of any major chord is 1½ steps (see "Whole Steps and Half Steps," p. 103).

QUESTIONS

3. The scale tone upon which a chord is built is called the
   _____ of the chord.

4. Each chord contains a _____, a _____, and
   a _____.

5. The fifth of the chord is located _____ letters up the
   musical alphabet from the root.

6. There is a musical interval of _____ steps between the
   root and the third of any major chord.

7. Between the third and the fifth of any major chord is an interval of _____ steps.

Answers p. 297

Each one of these chords is numbered according to its position in the scale sequence. A chord built on the first tone of the scale (with DO as the root) is called the I chord—also known as the *tonic* chord. A chord built on the fourth tone of the scale (with FA as the root) is the IV chord. A chord built on the fifth tone of the scale (with SOL as the root) is the V chord.

Note syllable:	DO	RE	MI	FA	SOL	LA	TI	DO
Note number:	1	2	3	4	5	6	7	8
Chord number	I	ii	iii	IV	V	vi	vii	I

┌─ QUESTIONS ───┐

8. The I chord is built on the _____ tone of the major scale.

9. The I chord is also known as the _____ chord.

10. FA is always the root of the _____ (chord number) chord.

11. The root of the I chord is always _____ (syllable name).

Answers p. 297

└───┘

Tonic, Subdominant, and Dominant Chords

A triad or chord may be built on any note of the scale in any key. The most commonly used chords are those built on:

DO—the first tone of the scale
FA—the fourth tone of the scale
SOL—the fifth tone of the scale

These are the I, IV, and V chords, respectively, and are also known by the names *tonic* (I), *subdominant* (IV), and *dominant* (V). In the key of C they would be written on the staff as follows:

Tonic Subdominant Dominant
I   IV   V

In the key of F they are written:

Tonic Subdominant Dominant
I   IV   V

In the key of G:

Tonic Subdominant Dominant
I   IV   V

QUESTIONS

12. The most commonly used chords are those built on the _____, _____, and _____ tones of the scale.

13. The name of the IV chord is the _____; the name of the V chord is the _____.

14. Construct a triad over each root note shown below:

Answers p. 297

Seventh Chords

Chords may contain more than three tones. When a fourth tone is added seven notes above the root, the chord becomes known as a "seventh" chord. The most common seventh chord is built on the dominant (fifth) tone of the scale and is called the *dominant seventh* chord. Seventh chords are written with the figure 7 next to the chord number, e.g., V7. The interval between the 5th of the V7 chord and the added 7th tone is 1½ steps.

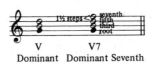

V   V7
Dominant   Dominant Seventh

The root of the dominant seventh chord is the same as that of the dominant chord—the fifth scale tone SOL.

QUESTIONS

15. A seventh chord contains _____ (number) tones.

16. The interval between the fifth of the chord and the added seventh is _____ steps.

17. The V7 chord is known as the _____ _____ chord.

18. _____ (scale syllable name) is the root of the V7 chord as well as the _____ chord.

19. Transform each of the following triads into seventh chords:

Answers p. 297

Chord Syllables

A breakdown of the syllables of each chord in the foregoing keys reveals that:

> The syllables of the I chord are always DO MI SOL
> The syllables of the IV chord are always FA LA DO
> The syllables of the V chord are always SOL TI RE
> The syllables of the V7 chord are always SOL TI RE FA

These facts hold true in the keys shown as well as in *all* keys, providing a basis for creating simple harmonies to given melodies (see p. 261).

QUESTIONS

20. DO MI and SOL are the notes of the _____ chord.
21. FA is contained in the IV chord and also in the _____ chord.
22. The tone common to both the I chord and the V chord is _____ (syllable).
23. The tone contained in the V7 chord but not contained in the V chord is _____ (syllable).

Answers pp. 297–298

Chord Letter Names

In addition to being referred to by number, chords are also called by letter names. These letter names are derived from the *root* upon which the chord is built.

QUESTIONS

24. Chords may be designated by _____ as well as by numbers.
25. Chord letter names are derived from the _____ of each chord.

Answers p. 298

If the root of the chord is C, the letter name for that chord is C. If the root is F, the chord letter name is F.

QUESTIONS

26. In the key of C the root of the I chord is _____ (letter name).

27. The chord letter name is F when the root of the chord is _____.

Answers p. 298

If the root of the chord is G, then the chord letter name is G. If there is an added seventh in the chord, then the chord letter name must also have the number 7 added, as shown in the example below:

QUESTIONS

28. G is the root of the V chord in the key of _____.

29. The chord letter name of the V7 chord in the key of C would be _____.

30. Write the chord *letter names* above the staff corresponding to each of the Roman numerals according to the key signature shown:

31. Write the *chord numbers* below the staff corresponding to each of the chord letters according to the key signature shown:

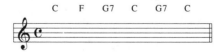

Answers p. 298

Shown below are the I, IV, V and V7 chords in a key other than C. Note that a new key means a new letter name for the I or tonic chord from which all other chord numbers and letters must be reckoned accordingly:

KEY OF F

I   IV   V   V7

Tonic Subdominant Dominant Dominant Seventh

In the key of F the root of the I chord is F (DO); thus the chord letter name for the I chord in the key of F is *F*. Beginning with F as *one* and counting up four letters of the musical alphabet in this key, the root of the IV chord falls on B♭ (FA) and the root of the V chord on C (SOL). When a V7 chord is indicated, the chord letter name must be accompanied by the figure 7 as shown (C7 — V and V7 chords share the same root):

KEY OF F

F   B♭   C   C7

I   IV   V   V7

QUESTIONS

32. In the key of F the root of the I chord is _____ (letter name).

33. The B♭ chord in the key of F is the _____ (I, IV, V7) chord.

34. The V7 chord in the key of F is written _____ (B♭, G, C7, F).

35. Write the chord *letter names* above the staff corresponding to each of the Roman numerals according to the key signature shown:

I   IV   I   IV   V7   I

36. Write the *chord numbers* below the staff corresponding to each of the chord letters according to the key signature shown:

F   C7   F   B♭   C7   F

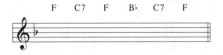

Answers p. 298

In the key of G the root of the I chord is G, thus the chord letter name for that chord is G. Four letters up the musical alphabet from G is C, the root of the IV chord. The tone D is the root of the V chord as well as the V7. When a V7 chord is indicated the chord letter must be written *D7*.

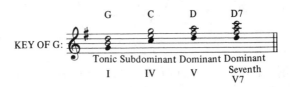

QUESTIONS

37. The chord letter name of the V7 chord in the key of G is

    _____.

38. C is the chord letter name of the _____ chord in the key of G.

39. Write the *chord letter names* over each of the given Roman numerals below according to the key signature shown.

40. Write the *chord numbers* below the staff corresponding to each of the chord letters according to the key signature shown:

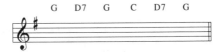

Answers p. 298

TRANSPOSING CHORDS

When transposing a song from one key to a different key (see "Transposition," p. 129), the chord letters shown for the given song must also be transposed into those suitable for the new key if harmony is to be added. For example, the song excerpt below shows chord letters for the key of C.

Inversions

When chords are written and sounded in the manner shown below, that is, with the root (scale tone upon which the chord is built) occurring in the *lowest* position, they are in what is known as the *root position:*

Sometimes chords are written and sounded in positions other than the root position. These are known as *inversions*. When the third of the chord appears in the lowest position, it is the *first inversion*. When the fifth of the chord appears in the lowest position, it is the *second inversion*. In the example below, the notes of the tonic chord in C (C E G) remain the same—only their position is changed.

Root
position

First
inversion

Second
inversion

Any chord in any key may be used in an inverted position.

QUESTIONS

43. When a chord is written with the root occurring in the lowest position, the chord is said to be in _____ position.
44. A chord written in other than root position is an _____.
45. In the first inversion the _____ of the chord is in lowest position.
46. When the fifth of the chord is in the lowest position, it is the _____ inversion.

Answers p. 298

Inversions are frequently used to facilitate smoother chord progressions either vocally or instrumentally.

┌─ QUESTIONS ───

47. Smoother progressions are facilitated by the use of _____.
48. Indicate whether the chords shown below are written in root position or inverted positions (note key signatures):

Answers p. 298

Minor Chords

A major chord may be transformed into a minor chord by simply lowering the third of the chord a half step:

The resulting minor sound stems from the fact that the distance from the root to the third of the chord (although still 3 letters apart on the musical alphabet) is now reduced from the previous major third interval of 2 whole steps to a minor third interval of 1½ steps.

┌─ QUESTIONS ───

49. A major chord may be made minor by _____ the third of the chord _____ step.
50. A major third interval consists of two _____ steps; a minor third interval consists of _____ steps.
51. Transform the following given major triads into minor triads:

Answers p. 298

The principal chords in minor keys are built on the 1st, 4th and 5th tones of the minor scale (chords below are shown in the natural minor form):

Minor chords take their names from chord roots as they did in the major.

QUESTIONS

52. The principal triads in a minor key are built on the _____, _____ and _____ tones of the scale.

53. The I chord in the key of d minor would be built on the note _____.

54. The root of the V chord in the key of f minor would be the note _____.

55. A minor chord built on the tone F would be called _____.

Answers p. 298

(See Minor Chords in "Additional Piano Chords for Left Hand," p. 259.)

Cadences

Cadences represent the stopping or pausing places in music. The feeling of completeness or final resolution that occurs at the end of many pieces of music is very often due to the use of the V7–I (or V–I) chord progression. The V7–I (or V–I) is known as an *authentic* or *complete cadence*.

The progression I–V7 (or I–V) is a *half cadence* and is more pause than stop. Hearing this progression nearly always indicates that there is more to come. A half cadence usually occurs somewhere in the middle of a song, somewhat like a comma in the middle of a sentence. The IV–I progression is known as a *plagal cadence* and is commonly heard in the closing "Amen" of many hymns.

QUESTIONS

56. Stopping or pausing places in music are known as _____.

57. The progression I to V7 or I to V is a _____ cadence.

58. A half cadence in music may be likened to a _____ in a sentence.
59. A complete or full cadence is the chord progression _____ to _____.
60. The progression IV–I is known as a _____ cadence.

Answers p. 298

CREATING HARMONY

Chord Root Harmony

Knowledge of chord structure enables one to add harmony to a given melody through the use of various simple devices such as chord roots, for example. In *chord root* harmony one group of voices sings or plays the melody while another group sings or plays the *root note* of each chord indicated in the song as it appears. When the chords in the song are limited to I, IV, and V7 (or V), the choice of root chording notes is limited to DO, FA, and SOL since these are the root note syllables of the I, IV, and V7 (or V) chords, respectively.

QUESTIONS

61. Simple harmony may be made by having one group of voices sing the melody while another group sings the _____ of each chord.
62. DO is the root chording syllable for the _____ chord.
63. The root chording syllable for the IV chord is _____.
64. The root chording syllable for the V chord is the same as it is for the _____ chord.

Answers p. 299

To find the appropriate root chording note, first determine the key of the song, then, calling the keynote *one,* count up the musical alphabet to the letter name of the next chord shown. If the fourth letter is the letter name of the chord, then the IV chord is indicated and the root syllable for that chord would be FA. If the count needed to reach the letter name of the chord is five, then the V or V7 chord is indicated and the root syllable for that chord would be SOL.

QUESTIONS

65. The root syllable of the IV chord is found by counting up _____ from the keynote of the song.

66. When counting up to find the root chording syllable, the keynote of the song should always be counted as _____.

Answers p. 299

In the song shown below, G is the I or tonic chord since the song is in the key of G. Whenever the chord letter G appears over a measure of the song that measure is to be harmonized with the I or tonic chord. The root of the tonic or I chord is always DO; thus DO would be the root chording syllable for every letter G appearing in this song. D7 represents the V7 chord in this key because D is five up from G in the musical alphabet; thus SOL would be the root chording syllable for all D7 chords shown.

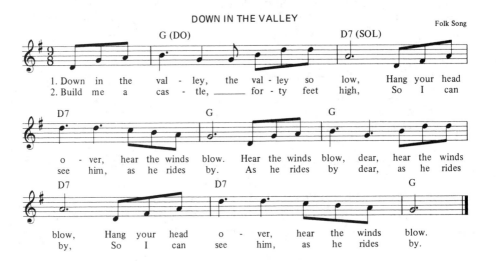

DOWN IN THE VALLEY

Folk Song

QUESTIONS

67. Does the song above contain any chord other than I and V7?

68. If the song contained a IV chord what chord letter name would appear?

69. What root chording syllable would be sung for the IV chord?

70. In the key of G the tonic chord is indicated by the letter _____ and the root syllable for the tonic chord is _____.

71.   In the musical alphabet, D is five up from _____.

Answers p. 299

In determining the root chording syllables for a song in a different key (F in the example below), note that all chord letters must be reckoned from the keynote F as *one*. B♭ would represent the fourth tone of the scale and C the fifth tone; thus B♭ denotes the IV chord in this key and C7 the V7 chord:

In summary:

Key of F

Chord letter	Chord number	Root chording syllable
F	I	DO
B♭	IV	FA
C7	V7	SOL

QUESTIONS

72.   Determine the root chording syllables for each of the chords in the following song excerpt:

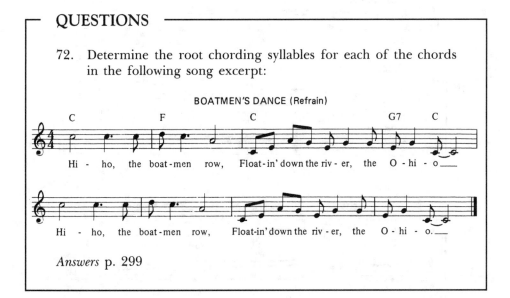

Answers p. 299

Ostinato

An *ostinato* is a repeated melodic fragment that may also be sounded against a given melody to produce a very simple form of harmony. In choosing the appropriate tones for an ostinato, as in choosing tones for a descant, the structure of the chords specified for each measure or section of the song must be considered. Some songs can conceivably be harmonized with just one chord, thus the ostinato could remain the same throughout the song. For example, in "Row, Row, Row Your Boat" (p. 67) it is possible to sing or play just DO SOL as an ostinato all the way through, singing the words "Row, row" or any others desired on the two notes. (The ostinato must be in the same key as the song.)

The same is true of "Are You Sleeping," using a three-note ostinato on the words "Brother John" or "Ding Ding Dong":

A more melodically interesting ostinato may be found in the song below.

ZUM GALI GALI

An ostinato may also be rhythmic, consisting of a rhythm pattern repeated over and over throughout the musical selection. The following ostinatos may be played with the song "Zum Gali Gali" above.

DESCANTS

Knowledge of chord structure also enables the writing of original *descants* for selected songs. The simple American folk song "Skip to My Lou" is used here to illustrate the process.

Descants are conceived from notes contained in the chord specified for a given measure of a song. "Skip to My Lou" is in the key of F, thus the chord letter F shown over the first two measures represents the I chord in this key and indicates tonic (I) chord harmony. The I chord contains DO MI SOL; thus, any one of these notes may be selected as descant tones for the first two measures of the song. Since there is no SOL in the melody in the first measure, it has been chosen here for the first descant note, with MI as the second note. Satisfactory harmony is anticipated since SOL and MI will fall an interval of a third above the melody notes. For smoother flow, two half notes have been used against the four quarter notes of the melody rhythm:

Chord letter C7 over the third and fourth measures specifies the V7 chord, thus the notes of the descant must change to include those of the V7 chord— SOL TI RE or FA. Since the melody notes are RE RE TI TI, FA has been chosen as another acceptable harmonization in thirds with the RE of the melody and an easy voice progression from the MI of the second measure. When the melody descends to TI, the descant moves to RE—a simple skip from the previous FA.

The melody in measures 5–8 is the same as that in measures 1–4. This allows the descant to repeat also, with one exception—SOL replaces RE in the seventh measure to avoid the none too harmonious sound of RE falling on the accented beat with MI in the melody. From SOL it is a simple drop down to MI for the final note to harmonize with DO of the melody. When completed, the descant shapes up as follows (it may be played or sung with the song shown):

SKIP TO MY LOU

It should be noted that the chord tones used in a descant fall on the *accented* beats of each measure. Tones not contained in a specified chord (*non-*

chord tones) are sometimes used in descants; however, they should fall on *unaccented* beats for more acceptable sound. Descants may be written with as few as one note for each measure or as many as desired, depending on the meter signature, keeping in mind that the tones on the accented beats should be those contained in the specified chord.

Harmony in Thirds and Sixths

Some songs, such as "Polly Wolly Doodle," lend themselves to simple harmonization by adding a part an interval of a third above the melody:

Oh, I   went down south for to   see   my   Sal etc.

Others sound better with the third added *below* the melody:

Du,   du   liegst mir   im   Her - zen, etc.

Harmonizing in this manner will not work for all songs; however, it is possible to find portions of certain songs that may be adapted, such as the section of "Down in the Valley" shown below:

Hear the wind blow

Some tunes harmonize well with a part added an interval of a sixth below the melody:

STANDIN' IN THE NEED OF PRAYER

Spiritual

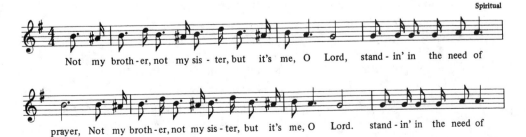

Not my broth-er, not my sis - ter, but   it's me, O   Lord,   stand - in' in   the need of

prayer, Not my broth-er, not my sis - ter, but   it's me, O   Lord.   stand - in' in   the need of

prayer. It's a - me, it's me, it's me, O Lord,   stand - in' in   the need of

prayer. It's a - me, it's me, it's me, O Lord,   stand - in in   the need of prayer.

Here again, not every song can be adapted to harmonizing in this way.

Vocal Chording

Vocal chording is the sounding of chordal accompaniment by voice rather than instrument. Three groups of voices are used, with each group sounding one of the tones contained in each of the I, IV and V7 chords. (The fifth of the V7 chord, RE, is omitted in order to accommodate the three-voice limit.) By using the IV and V7 chords in inverted positions (see p. 212) and the I chord in root position, common tones may be held over as they occur, with all other moves stepwise. This simplifies voice progression and results in a smoother sound:

GROUP 3 sings	SOL	LA	SOL	SOL	SOL
GROUP 2 sings	MI	FA	MI	FA	MI
GROUP 1 sings	DO	DO	DO	TI	DO
Chords:	I	IV	I	V7	I

Note that no group sings more than two different tones, and that the movement of the voices is the same as that of the fingers in left hand block chording on the piano. (See p. 241.)

A solo voice, several voices or an instrument may be used to sound the melody while the other voices provide the vocal three-part harmony accompaniment.

To find the appropriate Roman numeral in a given song, simply translate the chord letter names shown into numerals using the keynote (DO) as *one*. Obviously, at the outset songs will be limited to any that may be harmonized with the I, IV, and V7 chords, but even those are many, and the same principle may be applied when other chords are desired.

QUESTIONS

73. The sounding of chords vocally rather than instrumentally is known as _____ _____.

74. Smoother voice progressions are made possible by holding over the _____ _____ in each chord.

75. The I chord always contains _____, _____, _____ (syllables).

76. LA is contained only in the _____ chord.

77. To harmonize RE, the _____ (I, IV, V7) chord must be used.

78. The common tone in the I and IV chords is _____.

79. SOL is the common tone in the _____ and _____ chords.

80. _____ is contained in both the IV and the V7 chords.

Answers p. 299

The arrangement for "Silent Night" shown below illustrates how vocal chording accompaniment appears when written on the staff in notation. Group I would sing the lowest note of each chord, Group II, the middle note, and Group III the highest note. Chord tones may be hummed or sung on a neutral syllable such as "oo" or "ah."

SILENT NIGHT

Music by Franz Gruber
Words translated by John F. Young
from the German by Joseph Mohr

VOCAL CHORDING FOR *SILENT NIGHT*

Part Singing

Choirs, glee clubs, and other vocal groups whose musical pursuits transcend simple harmonic devices such as partner songs and vocal chording draw their repertoire from song material specially arranged for various voice combinations.

A two-part arrangement for *soprano* and *alto* voices is designated *SA*, a three-part arrangement for *first* and *second soprano* and *alto* voices *SSA*, and a four-part arrangement for *first* and *second soprano* and *first* and *second alto* *SSAA*, with choice depending on whether the ability of the group extends to two, three or four parts. The soprano voice is higher than the alto and frequently, although not always, carries the melody.

In a male group the voices are classified *tenor, baritone,* and *bass,* with the bass as the lowest voice and the first tenor the highest. When arranged for four parts the designation is *TTBB—first tenor, second tenor, first bass* (or baritone) and *second bass.* Two- and three-part arrangements for tenor and bass combinations are also available for male voices.

QUESTIONS

81. SSA stands for _____, _____ and _____.
82. The alto voice sounds _____ (higher, lower) than the soprano.
83. The designation for first and second soprano and first and second alto is _____.
84. The highest voice in an all-male group is the _____ _____.
85. TTBB stands for _____, _____, _____ and _____.

Answers p. 299

A *mixed chorus* contains male and female voices. Four-part arrangements for such groups are designated *SATB—soprano, alto, tenor,* and *bass*—for the most part; however, other voice combinations, such as *SAB*—soprano, alto and baritone—are also used.

QUESTIONS

86. In a mixed chorus the female voices are usually assigned the _____ and _____ parts.

87. The lowest male voice is the _____.

88. SATB stands for _____, _____, _____, _____.

89. SAB stands for _____, _____, _____.

Answers p. 299

Examples of various vocal groupings are represented in the songs that follow. Note that the staves are joined in sets of two or more by a connecting vertical line, indicating that whatever is written on each of the connected staves is to be sung simultaneously to produce the harmony.

In "Sinner Man" below, the soprano part is written on the *upper* staff of each set of the two joined staves, while the alto part is written on the *lower* staff of each set of two.

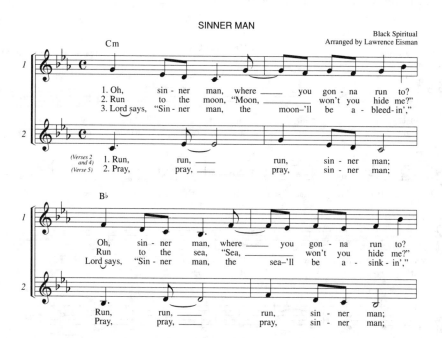

SINNER MAN

Black Spiritual
Arranged by Lawrence Eisman

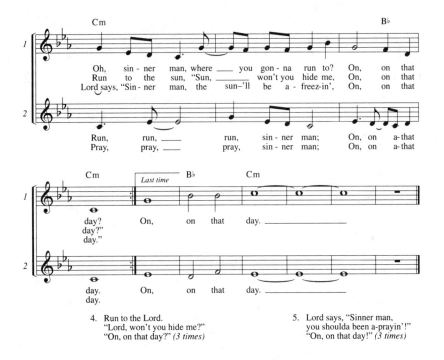

4. Run to the Lord.
   "Lord, won't you hide me?"
   "On, on that day?" *(3 times)*

5. Lord says, "Sinner man,
   you shoulda been a-prayin'!"
   "On, on that day!" *(3 times)*

In "Chopsticks" and "Let Us Break Bread Together" (both SSA) the first soprano part is written on the upper staff, the second soprano and alto parts on the lower staff, of each set of two staves.

CHOPSTICKS

Words and descant by DIANA CHRISTY

LET US BREAK BREAD TOGETHER

Spiritual (arranged by William S. Haynie)

Reverently

1. Let us break bread to-geth-er on our knees, _____ Let us
2. Let us praise God to-geth-er on our knees, _____ Let us

on our knees,
on our knees,

break bread to-geth-er on our knees _____ When I fall on my
praise God to-geth-er on our knees _____

on our knees. When I fall on my
on our knees.

knees with my face to the ris-ing sun, Oh, Lord, have mer-cy on me. _____

knees with my face to the ris-ing sun, Oh, Lord, have mer-cy on _ me, on me.

Don't for-get the tune and rhy-thm
One tune up, the oth-er down, _____ down,

Be sure to give them that reg-u-lar rhy-thm and

Ev-'ry-bod-y likes and knows.
That's the way that "Chop-sticks" goes.

har-mo-ny ev-'ry-one likes and knows.

In "Cockles and Mussels" (SAB) the soprano and alto parts are on the upper staff, with the baritone part on the lower.

COCKLES AND MUSSELS

Irish Folk Song
Arr. by Buryl A. Red

In "Promised Land" the soprano part is on the upper staff, the alto on the middle staff, and the tenor and bass on the lower staff. Note that harmony begins on the *refrain*.

THE PROMISED LAND

Camp Meeting Song
Arranged by James W. Rodger

1. On Jor-dan's storm-y banks I stand And cast a wish-ful eye. To ___ Ca-naan's fair and hap-py land Where my pos-ses-sions lie.
2. There gen-erous fruits that nev-er fail On trees im-mor-tal grow; There rocks and hills and brooks and vales With milk and hon-ey flow. I am
3. No chill-ing winds nor poison-ous breath Can reach that health-ful shore; Sick-ness and sor-row, pain and death Are felt and feared no more. I am
4. When shall I reach that hap-py place And be for-ev-er blest? When shall I see my Fa-ther's face, And in His bos-om rest?

Oh,

bound for the prom-ised land, ___ I'm bound for the prom-ised land. Oh, ___

who will come and go with me, Oh, who will come and go with me, Oh,

rit. last time

who will come and go with me? I am bound for the prom-ised land.

who will come and go with me? I'm bound for the prom-ised land.

In "Good Night, Ladies" the soprano and alto parts are shown on the upper staff, tenor and bass parts on the lower. This particular arrangement contains chromatic tones that give the harmony a "barbershop" flavor.

"Doo-Bee" uses one staff for each voice group of the SATB arrangement.

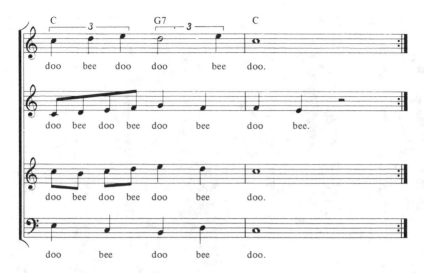

Accommodating choral arrangements written for six, eight, or more parts is accomplished by subdividing within each section of sopranos, altos, tenors, and basses.

ORCHESTRAL HARMONY

The symphony orchestra is often described as being made up of *choirs*, with each choir making its own harmony, as it were, through the various instruments playing the soprano, alto, tenor, and bass parts.

Strings (See illustration on p. 232)

The largest of these groups is the string choir, consisting of violins, violas, cellos, and bass viols.

The *violin* is the highest sounding instrument of the string choir and therefore could be considered the soprano of the group, with the slightly larger and lower *viola* frequently assigned the alto part. Although the *cello*, also called the violoncello, is actually the tenor of the string choir, it is frequently heard playing melody parts. The bass viol is the largest and lowest sounding instrument of the string choir. It is also referred to as *double bass, string bass, bass fiddle,* and just plain *bass.*

QUESTIONS

90. The symphony orchestra is made up of ___CHOIRS___ of instruments.

91. The largest choir of the symphony orchestra is the **STRING** choir.

92. The highest sounding string instrument is the ___VIOLIN___.

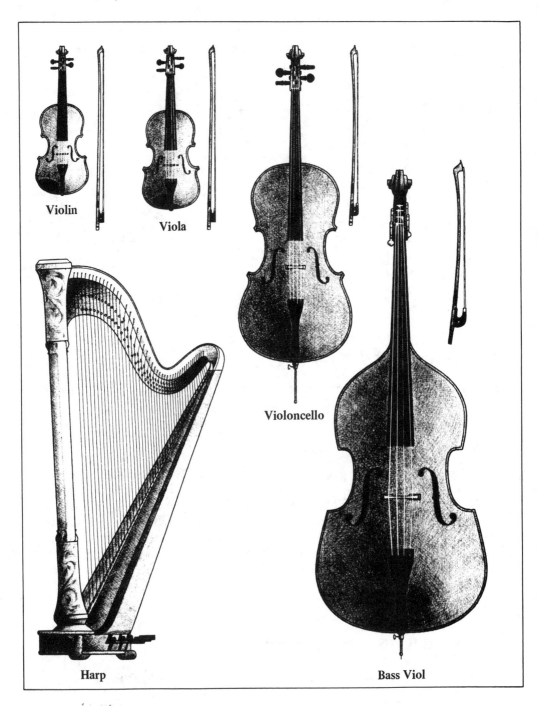

Violin

Viola

Violoncello

Harp

Bass Viol

93. The viola is considered the ___ALTO___ voice of the string choir.
94. The largest instrument of the string choir is the ___BASS___.

Answers p. 299

The violin, viola, cello (violoncello), and bass viol (double bass) are all played by drawing a *bow* over the strings. For a different musical effect, strings may be plucked as well as bowed. This plucking is known as *pizzicato*.

The *harp* is also considered to be a member of the string section of the orchestra; however, it is played only by plucking and not with a bow.

QUESTIONS

95. All instruments in the string choir except the ___HARP___ are played with a bow.
96. *Pizzicato* means ___PLUCKING___.
97. The smaller the instrument, the (higher, lower) it sounds.

Answers p. 299

Woodwinds (See illustration on p. 234)

The woodwind choir makes its sounds by blowing rather than bowing. The *piccolo* is tiny and high sounding—in fact, the highest sounding instrument of all the woodwinds. The *flute* is less shrill and slightly lower in range. Both the piccolo and the flute are held to the side, and played by blowing across an opening to make the sound. Various keys are pressed down to change the pitches of the tones. Piccolos and flutes have no reeds.

QUESTIONS

98. Woodwind instruments are played by ___BLOWING___.
99. The ___PICCOLO___ is the highest sounding instrument of the woodwind choir.
100. The piccolo and the ___FLUTE___ are held and played in the same manner. These two instruments have no ___REEDS___.

Answers p. 299

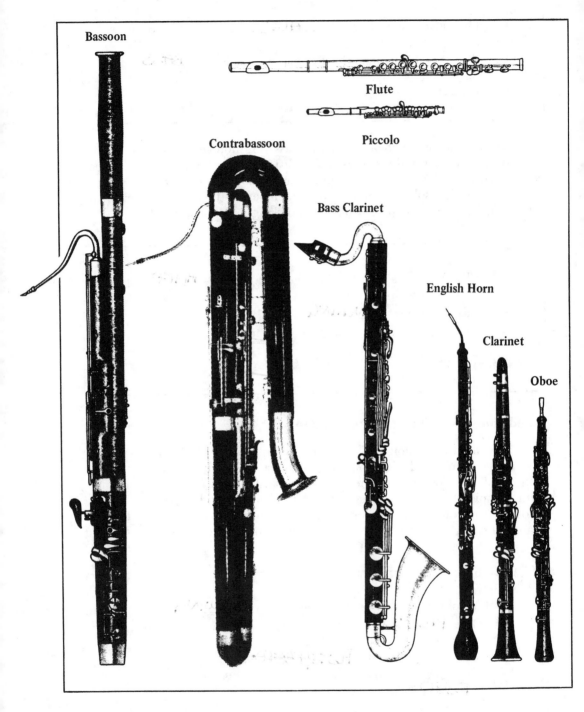

Bassoon

Flute

Contrabassoon

Piccolo

Bass Clarinet

English Horn

Clarinet

Oboe

The remainder of the woodwinds are divided into two classes according to the number of *reeds* (thin pieces of cane) used.

The *single reed* instruments are those on which a single piece of cane rests next to a mouthpiece. These include the *clarinet* and the larger and lower sounding *bass clarinet*. The *saxophone* is heard more in bands than in orchestras, although some composers have written symphonic works that have included saxophones in the scores. Since the mouthpiece of the saxophone is very similar to that of the clarinet, the saxophone would fall in the *single reed* category.

The *double reed* instruments are those on which the mouthpiece consists of two pieces of cane wired together. This gives them a rather distinctive tone quality or *timbre* reminiscent of the Middle East that we sometimes tend to associate with "snake charmer" music. Although some of the double reed instruments play in lower registers than others, the quality of the tone remains the same. The *oboe* is considered the "soprano" of the double reed group. The tone quality of the *English horn* is very much like that of the oboe, but the range is slightly lower, comparable to the alto voice. The *bassoon* is even lower, and larger of course, but it still retains the same kind of tone quality as the oboe and the English horn. The *contrabassoon* is the largest and lowest of all.

Whether single reed, double reed, or no reed, all woodwind instruments are played by blowing and pressing down keys.

QUESTIONS

101. Two classes of woodwind instruments are _SINGLE REED_ and _DOUBLE REED_

102. A clarinet is a _SINGLE_ reed instrument.

103. The soprano of the double reed instruments is the _OBOE_.

104. The largest of all the woodwind instruments is the _CONTRABASSOON_

Answers p. 299

Brass (See illustration on p. 236)

The brass choir consists of the *trumpet, French horn, trombone,* and *tuba* usually playing in the soprano, alto, tenor, and bass range, respectively. The sound is produced by pressing the lips against a mouthpiece and blowing into it while pressing down on a valve simultaneously. Since brass instruments have a limited number of valves, pitches are varied by tightening the lips for a higher pitch and loosening them for a lower one. On the trombone the

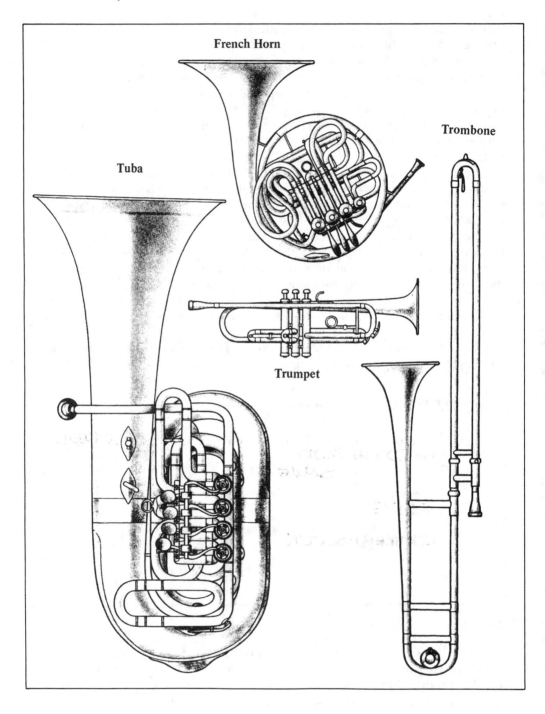

French Horn

Trombone

Tuba

Trumpet

change of pitch is dependent upon the movement of a slide in place of valves. The sound of the French horn is reminiscent of the hunting horns that it resembles and often portrays.

QUESTIONS

105. The trumpet belongs to the _BRASS_ choir of the orchestra.
106. The _FRENCH_ _HORN_ resembles and sounds like a hunting horn.
107. The brass instrument played by moving a slide in and out is a _TROMBONE_.
108. The _TUBA_ is the lowest-sounding brass instrument.
109. When playing certain brass instruments, pitches may be varied by _TIGHTENING_ or _LOOSENING_ the lips.

Answers pp. 299–300

Percussion (See illustration on p. 238)

The instruments that make up the percussion section of a symphony orchestra are those that are played for the most part by striking or shaking. Many of these instruments, including the *wood block, snare drum,* and *cymbals,* have no definite pitch. The *kettle drums* or *timpani* (TIM-pah-nee) may be tuned to desired pitches for the given piece being performed. Tunes may be played on *melodic percussion* instruments such as *xylophone, chimes, bells* and *celesta.* See illustration on p. 238.

QUESTIONS

110. Instruments that are played by striking or shaking are known as _PERCUSSION_ instruments.
111. _KETTLE DRUMS_ may be tuned to definite pitches.
112. Melodic percussion instruments include the _CHIMES_ and the _BELLS._

Answers p. 300

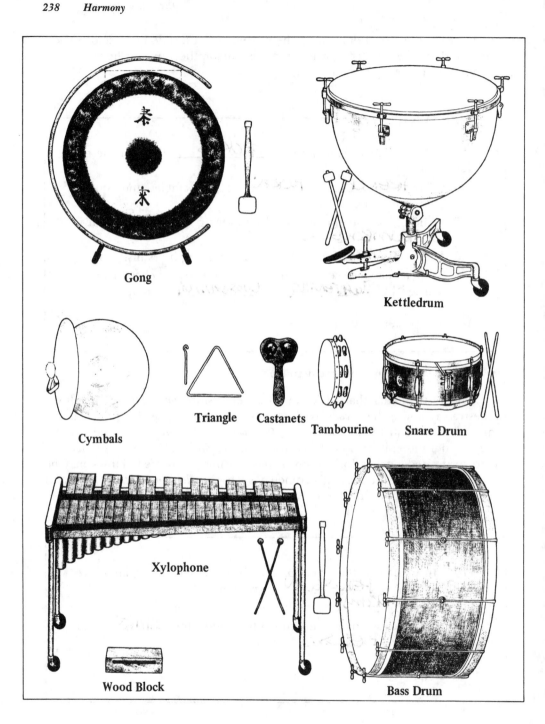

Gong

Kettledrum

Cymbals

Triangle   Castanets

Tambourine   Snare Drum

Xylophone

Wood Block

Bass Drum

Young Person's Guide to the Orchestra, by Benjamin Britten, presents fine examples of the sound of all instruments of the orchestra.

Identifying instruments of the orchestra by sight and sound is but one of several ways of increasing enjoyment when listening to large musical works performed by symphony orchestras. Another is by becoming familiar with various types of musical *form.*

FORM

The term "form" may have several different references in music. In one context, form may refer to a classification of a musical work; in another, it may mean the particular structure or design within that work as it relates to the arrangement of its musical content.

Symphonies, concertos, sonatas, and other similar musical works are classed as large musical forms, each containing several divisions known as *movements.* Within selected movements of each of these large forms there may be a designated type of musical structure also known as *form.* For example, a section of musical material termed *A,* followed by a contrasting section termed *B,* followed in turn by a repeat of the original *A* is known as *ABA,* or *ternary* form. These repetitions and contrasts are clearly delineated in *sonata form* under the designations of *exposition, development,* and *recapitulation,* rounded off by a small concluding section known as a *coda.*

Two-part form, called *binary,* is designated *AB* and contains a musical idea followed by a contrasting one but does not return to the *A* section as in ternary form.

Rondo form, represented by the letters *ABACA,* states a well-defined theme *(A)* at the outset, which then alternates with contrasting themes *(B* and *C)* and returns to conclude the piece.

Form may also be used to describe a particular way in which a given musical element such as melody, for example, is handled. A musical title containing the words "Theme and Variations" or simply "Variations" indicates that the listener may expect to hear a theme or melody subjected to various musical alterations (variations) such as a change of key, meter, mode, instrumentation, and/or other form of modification throughout the piece.

When the title designation is *fugue,* it means that a theme or melody will be introduced in one voice, then closely imitated in other voices entering at spaced intervals. Although comparable to a *round* in this respect, a fugue is far more complex in its musical structure.

The presence of form is not limited to large musical works. It may also be found in songs and other short pieces. *Strophic form* (or *strophic song form*) is a term applied to songs containing several stanzas wherein the words may vary but the music remains the same for each stanza, or *strophe.* When the music is *different* for every stanza, the form is known as *through composed.*

Certain forms that do not fall into any of the aforementioned categories are often referred to as *free forms* and may bear such titles as "Etude," 'Nocturne," "Fantasie," "Rhapsody," and others. It should be noted, however, that no matter how "free" a composition may sound, a composer, when manipulating musical elements, must still yield to some basic principles of organization.

PLAYING HARMONY ON A KEYBOARD INSTRUMENT

Harmony on a keyboard instrument (piano, organ, etc.) is usually played with the *left* hand from the bass clef while the *right* hand plays the melody from the treble clef. The playing of chordal progressions is considerably simplified when *inversions* are used. In Example A below, all the chords appear in root position. In Example B, the I chord is in root position, but inversions are used for the IV and V7 chords. Note in Example B how the movement of the left hand is minimized through the use of inversions, with what may be anticipated as resulting smoother sound.

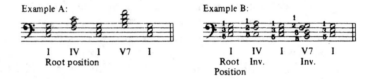

See "Left Hand Chording," p. 241.

Playing from the Bass Clef

Since the left hand usually plays from the bass clef, the introductory materials below are meant to provide practice in using the left hand as well as in reading notation from the bass clef prior to attempting chord progressions. Left hand fingers are numbered as follows:

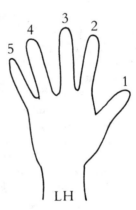

Left Hand Practice Melodies

Fingering for some of the tunes has been marked. In others it has been left unmarked to allow further practice for the player.

Left Hand Chording

The chord progressions shown below are written in bass clef and designed for left hand use.

To enable a player to move from one chord to another with a minimum of effort, the chords are arranged in *block* form. This means that the *tonic* (I) chord is always played in *root* position, while the *subdominant* (IV) and *dominant seventh* (V7) chords are played in inverted positions (see "Inversions," p. 212).

Note in the progression I–IV in the key of C shown below, the presence of the common tone C. By holding this tone over, the little finger is allowed to remain on C as the chord changes while the thumb and index finger each move up:

Key of C

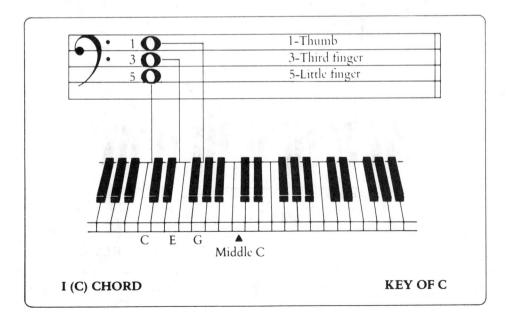

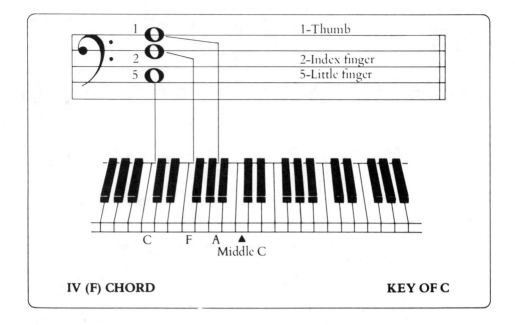

In the I to V7 progression, the *thumb* may remain where it is on the common tone G while the little finger moves down one and the index finger moves up one. The fifth of the V7 chord has been omitted to facilitate fingering; the effect of the V7 is the same even without the fifth.

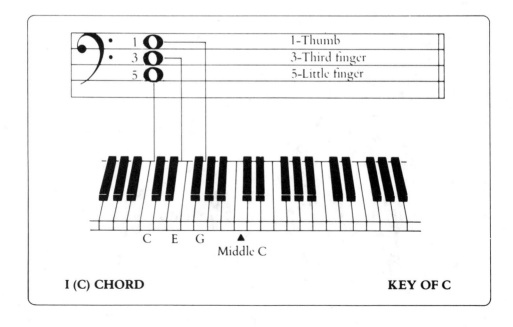

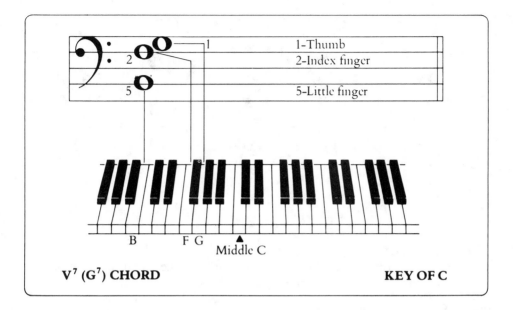

V⁷ (G⁷) CHORD   KEY OF C

Total progression for key of C

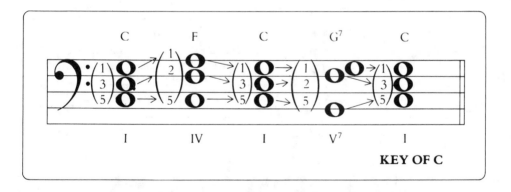

In the IV to V7 progression in the key of C shown below, note that the index finger remains stationary on the common tone (F) while the little finger and thumb each move *down* to the adjacent key. The finger movements shown for this progression are the same in *all keys*.

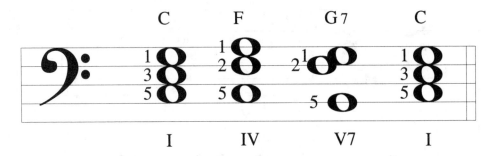

Although the chords shown below are in a different key than those on p. 243, the finger movements remain the same.

Key of F

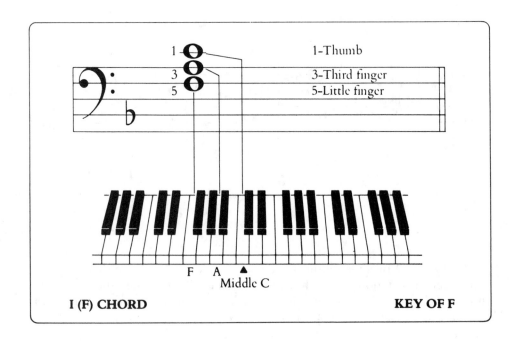

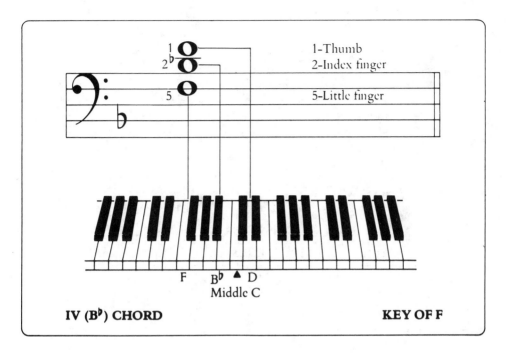

1-Thumb
2-Index finger
5-Little finger

F   B♭   ▲ D
Middle C

IV (B♭) CHORD   **KEY OF F**

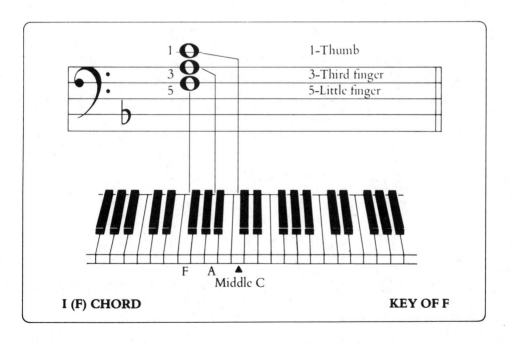

1-Thumb
3-Third finger
5-Little finger

F   A   ▲
Middle C

I (F) CHORD   **KEY OF F**

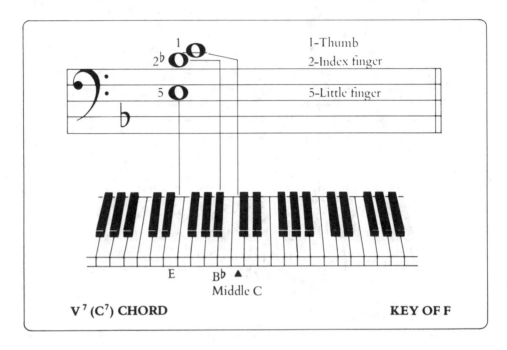

V⁷ (C⁷) CHORD   **KEY OF F**

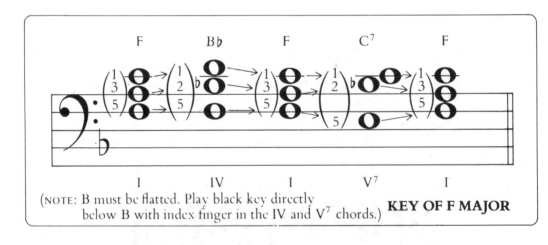

(NOTE: B must be flatted. Play black key directly
below B with index finger in the IV and V⁷ chords.)   **KEY OF F MAJOR**

In the IV to V7 progression in the key of F, the index finger remains stationary on the common tone (B♭) while the little finger and thumb each move
down to the adjacent keys.

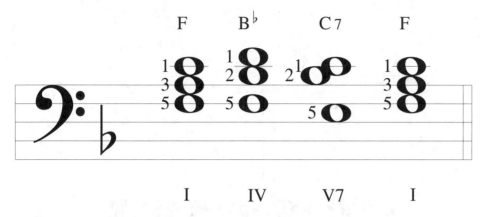

In the key of G below, note that the finger movements of the chord progressions remain the same as they were for the keys of C and F previously shown. The same holds true for all keys in which these progressions are used. (See "Additional Piano Chords for Left Hand," p. 258.)

Key of G

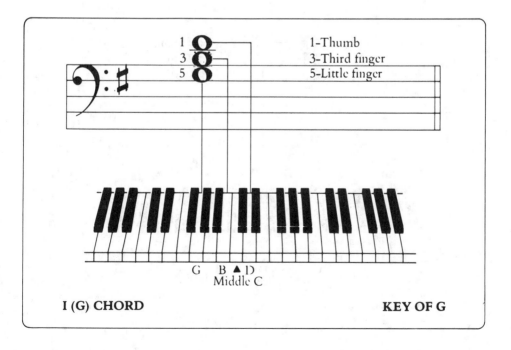

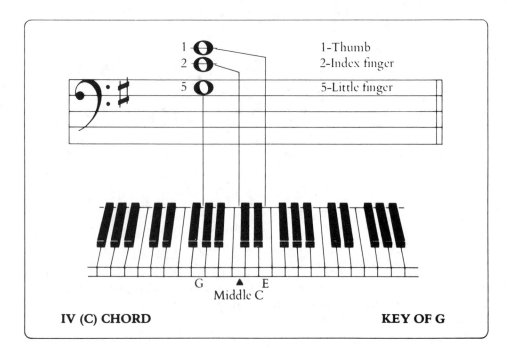

1 — Thumb
2 — Index finger
5 — Little finger

G   ▲   E
Middle C

IV (C) CHORD   **KEY OF G**

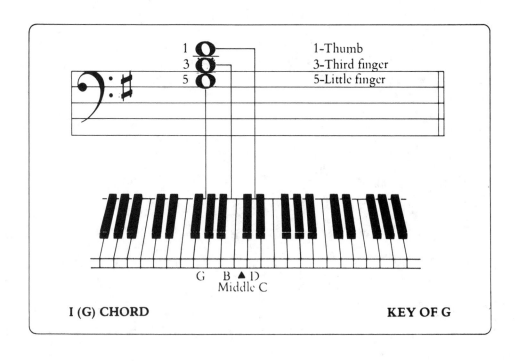

1 — Thumb
3 — Third finger
5 — Little finger

G   B ▲ D
Middle C

I (G) CHORD   **KEY OF G**

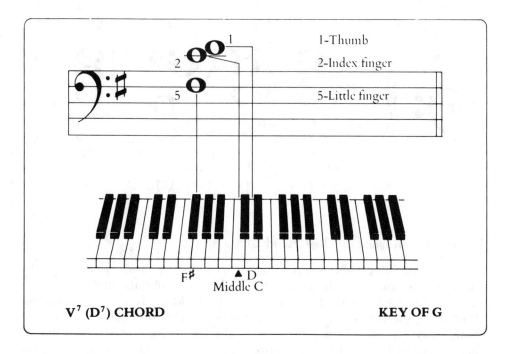

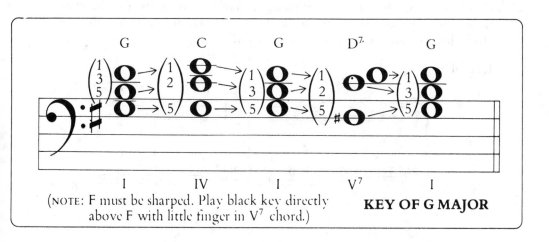

(NOTE: F must be sharped. Play black key directly above F with little finger in V⁷ chord.)　　**KEY OF G MAJOR**

In the IV to V7 progression in the key of G, the index finger remains stationary on the common tone (C) while the little finger and thumb each move down to the adjacent keys.

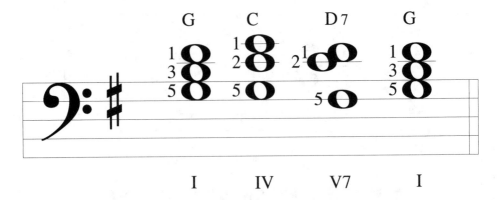

Practice Progressions for Left Hand Chording

The following short excerpts are designed to provide practice in the simultaneous use of both hands—the right hand playing melody, accompanied by the left hand playing chords. The melodies have been limited to those using the previously introduced five-note right hand position to enable more concentration on the movement of the left hand. It is assumed that as facility is gained in the left hand movement, the repertoire of songs will grow to include others outside the five-note range. Also, as skill increases in progressing from one chord to another in the left hand, the written bass clef chords may not be necessary. Since the hand movements are the same for these chord progressions in any key, the melody line alone with only the chord letters indicated above it may be sufficient.

Key of C

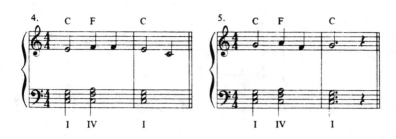

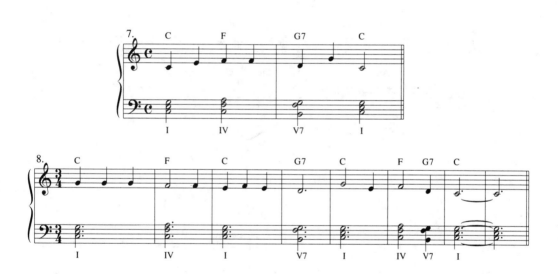

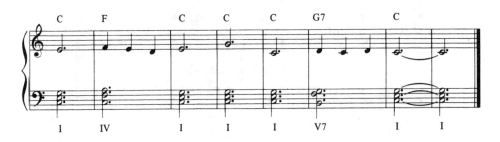

GO TELL AUNT RHODY

American Folk Song

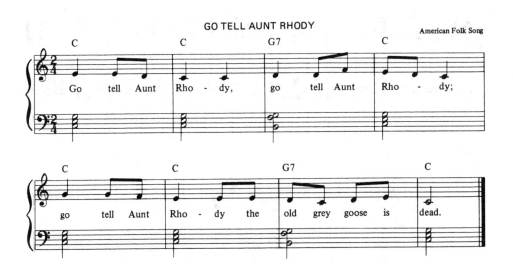

LIGHTLY ROW

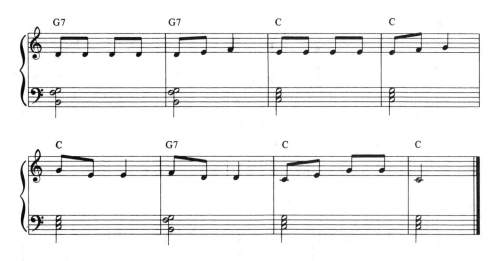

WHEN THE SAINTS GO MARCHING IN

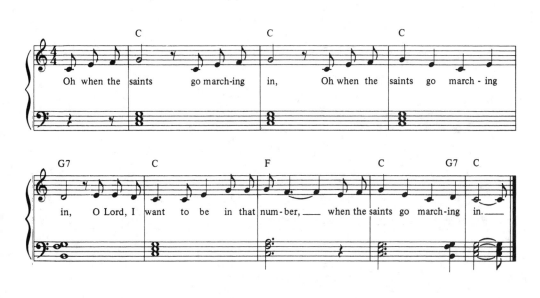

WHO'S THAT YONDER

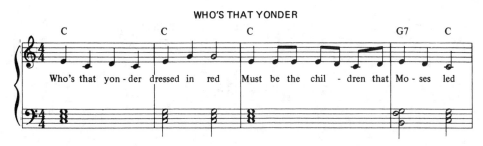

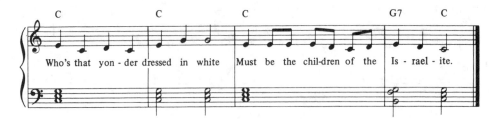

Who's that yon-der dressed in white   Must be the chil-dren of the   Is - rael - ite.

Key of F

LOVE SOMEBODY

AU CLAIR DE LA LUNE (excerpt)

A-HUNTING WE WILL GO

Oh a - hunt - ing we will go, a - hunt - ing we will go, We'll

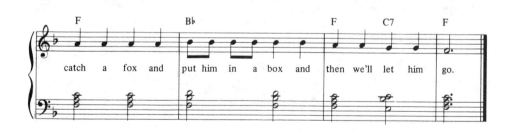

catch a fox and put him in a box and then we'll let him go.

Key of G

MERRILY WE ROLL ALONG

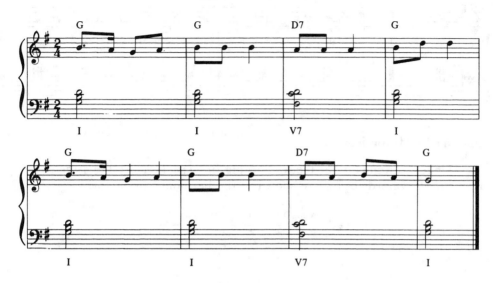

CRADLE SONG

ROUSSEAU

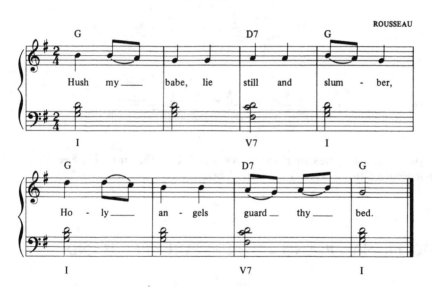

Hush my ___ babe, lie still and slum - ber,

Ho - ly ___ an - gels guard ___ thy ___ bed.

OATS PEAS BEANS

Oats peas beans and bar - ley grow   Oats peas beans and   bar - ley grow   Do

Playing in Minor Keys

Finger movements for block chording in *minor* keys are the same as for major (*Note:* Chords below are shown in the harmonic minor form):

For practice, see songs in minor keys pp. 182, 183, and 218. See also "Additional Piano Chords for Left Hand," below.

ADDITIONAL PIANO CHORDS FOR LEFT HAND

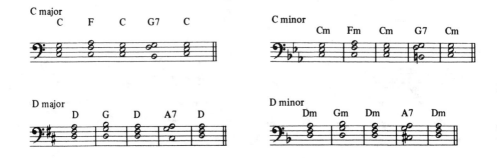

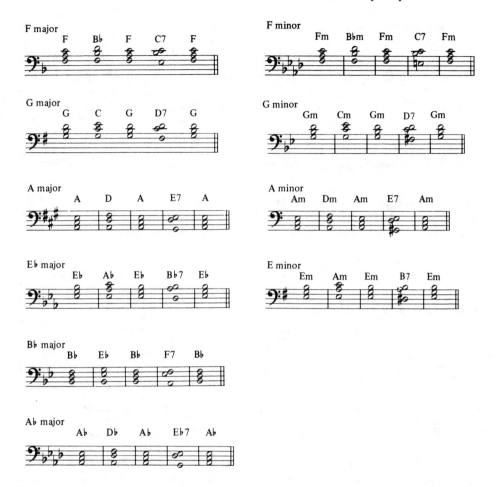

Left Hand Piano Accompaniment Styles

Left hand piano accompaniments are not limited to the block chording form suggested in the foregoing. They may vary in style. A chord may be broken into an *arpeggio* in which each tone of the chord is sounded separately in turn:

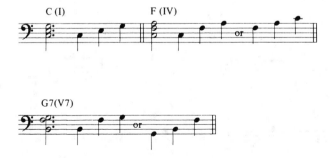

Note the use of this style in the song excerpt below.

A frequently used form of accompaniment is one in which the root of the chord is sounded on the strong beat with the remaining notes played together on the weak beats as shown in the excerpt of "Oh! Susanna" below:

When piano is used to accompany a melody being performed by another instrument or by voice, a completely rhythmic style may be used. In the excerpt of "Honey, You Can't Love One" shown below, note that the right hand is playing no melody, only chords:

What style of accompaniment would you choose for the song shown below?

There are numerous other styles of accompaniment; however, further exploration of these will be left to publications in which the emphasis is largely on acquiring keyboard skills.

Selecting Chords for Accompaniment

When chord letters or numerals are not indicated for a given song, it is possible to devise a simple accompaniment using I, IV, and V7 chords. Obviously, not all songs are adaptable to this limited chord selection; however, when additional chords are required, the principle involved in choosing them is the same—only the choices will be wider.

The following procedure is suggested for providing accompaniment for songs that may be harmonized with I, IV, and V7 chords:

A.   Locate DO in the song, then write the appropriate syllable names under the notes:

B.   Recall that:
     the I chord contains DO MI SOL,
     the IV chord contains FA LA DO, and
     the V7 chord contains SOL TI RE FA.

C.   Match the syllable names of the melody notes to those contained in the chords and insert the appropriate chord numeral under each syllable. For example, the first note MI in the song excerpt above is contained only in the I chord, thus the I chord should be used to harmonize MI. The second note RE is contained only in the V7 chord. The third note FA is found in both the IV and the V7 chords, permitting a choice. The fourth note MI dictates the I chord again; the fifth note LA and IV chord. The sixth note SOL again allows a choice between I and V7. The seventh tone RE calls for V7 again:

D.   Determine the letter names of the chords from the numerals according to the given key. As stated previously, chord letter names are derived from the root of the chord. In the key of F example below the root of the I chord is F; thus all I chords bear the letter name F, with letter names of the IV and V7 chords reckoned from F as *one*:

QUESTIONS

113. Was the I or tonic chord used to harmonize any tone of the scale other than DO? Which ones?

114. What chord may be used to harmonize both RE and TI?

115. The IV chord may be used to harmonize both _____ and _____.

116. The _____ of any given chord determines its letter name.

117. The chord letter name for the I chord in the key of C is _____.

118. In the key of F, B♭ is the chord letter name for the _____ (I, IV, V7) chord.

119. The chord letter name for the IV chord in the key of G is _____.

120. In the melody excerpt shown below:
    a. insert the appropriate chord numerals according to the procedure suggested (determining syllables, then recalling syllables found in each chord);
    b. write in the chord letter names based on the numerals. (When a choice occurs indicate numbers and letters of both possible chords.)

Answers p. 300

Chording every note of a song is not common practice, nor is it musically desirable. In most traditional songs, one or two chords usually suffice to serve a complete measure, depending on the notes of the melody and where the accents fall. When only one chord is shown for a whole measure in a song, it may be assumed that either all the melody notes in that measure are contained in the same chord or that most of them are—specifically, the ones that fall on the accented beats.

In the excerpt of the song shown below, RE is not contained in the I chord, to be sure, but it is rather insignificantly located on the *unaccented* beat of the measure surrounded by tones of the tonic chord; thus tonic chord (I) harmony is acceptable throughout the measure despite the presence of this *passing tone* foreign to the tonic chord. (A *passing tone* is defined as one moving stepwise between two chord tones in either an ascending or descending progression.) The same principle applies to the DO in the third measure.

Composing Melodies for Given Chord Progressions

A somewhat more creative pursuit relating to harmony is writing original melodies over given chord progressions such as the one shown below. Review the chord ingredients of the Roman numerals shown, then write in as few or as many melody notes as desired in each measure. These notes should fit within the structure of the given chords and may also include some passing tones. If the tune is to be sung, it should be noted that melodies moving stepwise or in small skip progressions are easier to sing than those with wide leaps and awkward intervals.

Chapter Ten

Chording Instruments

AUTOHARP

The *Autoharp* is considered among the easiest to play of the chording instruments because it makes harmony at the press of a button.

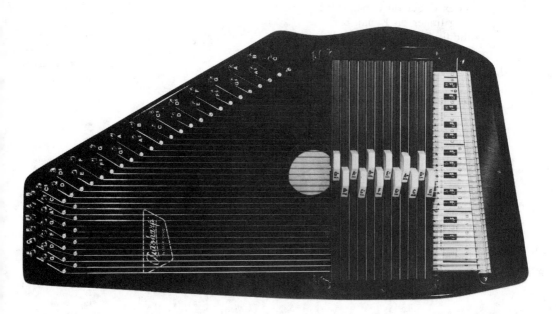

The arrangement of the chord bars enables the player to sound the principal chords (I, IV and V7) in given keys with adjacent fingers. The index finger plays the tonic (I) chord, the ring finger plays the subdominant (IV) chord and the middle finger plays the dominant seventh (V7) chord in each key. Following a little practice, the whole process may be accomplished by touch alone with no need to look at the chord bars.

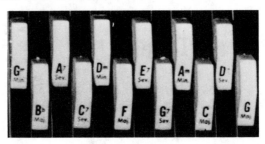

The fingers of the left hand press the chord bars while the right hand reaches across the left and strums. Chord bars must be pressed down firmly. Strumming on the left or wider side of the chord bars produces a fuller sound than strumming on the right or narrow side. The latter produces a banjolike effect. Various ways of strumming, including a two-directional movement, can produce a variety of rhythmic accompaniments.

For playing, the Autoharp should rest on a flat surface with the straight side closest to the player.

For the *key of C* (I, IV, and V7 chords):

Left Hand

Index finger on C major bar
Ring finger on F maj. bar
Middle finger on G7 bar

For the *key of F* (I, IV and V7 chords):

Left Hand

Index finger on F maj. bar (I)
Ring finger on B♭ maj. bar (IV)
Middle finger on C7 bar (V7)

For the *key of G* (I, IV and V7 chords):

Left Hand

Index finger on G maj. bar (I)
Ring finger on C maj. bar (IV)
Middle finger on D7 bar (V7)

Many songs may be accompanied by simply noting the chord letters indicated for the songs and pressing the corresponding chord bars on the Autoharp. Autoharps come in various models, depending on the number of chord bars. Those with twelve and fifteen bars are the most common, even though the number of keys in which one may play on them is limited to four. In recent years a twenty-one bar model has been developed that enables playing in many more keys. Electrified models are also available.

In the following songs Autoharp chords are indicated by letter names along with the stroke symbol / showing where to strum. These strumming patterns are only suggestions. As players become more familiar with the instrument they may devise their own ways of strumming.

POLLY WOLLY DOODLE   Key: F   Chords used: F–C7 Meter: $\frac{4}{4}$

```
     F/                      F/
Oh I went down South for to see my Sal
     F/                      C7/
Sing Polly Wolly Doodle all the day
  C7/          C7/
My Sal she is a spunky gal
  C7/                        F/
Sing Polly Wolly Doodle all the day
     F/           F/
Fare thee well, fare thee well
     F/           C7/
Fare thee well my fairy fay
  C7/                        C7/
For I'm off to Louisiana for to see my Susyanna
  C7/                        F/
Sing Polly Wolly Doodle all the day
```

KUM BA YAH   Key: C   Chords used: C–F–G7 Meter: $\frac{4}{4}$

```
     C/           F/    C/
Kum ba yah my Lord kum ba yah
     C/           F/    G7/
Kum ba yah my Lord kum ba yah
     C/           F/    C/
Kum ba yah my Lord kum ba yah
  F/  C/   G7/    C/
Oh Lord kum ba yah
```

Tuning the Autoharp   To insure accuracy, a pitch pipe or similar device should be used for tuning; however, if not available, or if the Autoharp is to be played in concert with other instruments such as recorder, bells, or piano, it may be tuned to those instruments. Included with all Autoharps is a hollow wrench used for adjusting the pitch of the string. Tightening the string produces a higher pitch, loosening the string results in a lower pitch. Players may choose from a variety of tuning procedures. The following are the most commonly used.

1. Tuning each string separately as it occurs in sequence.
2. Tuning by octaves (All E's, all F's, all G's, etc.)
3. Tuning by chords, making appropriate pitch adjustments where necessary, e.g.,
   a. Tune all F's, all A's, then all C's to sound the F chord.
   b. Tune all E's and G's to sound the C chord (C's previously tuned)
   c. Tune B's and D's to sound the G and G7 chords (other tones tuned previously)
   d. Tune all F♯s to sound D and D7 chords (other tones tuned previously)
   e. Tune all B♭s to sound the B♭ chord (other tones tuned previously)
   f. Tune all G♯s to sound the E7 chord (other tones tuned previously)
   g. Tune all C♯s to sound the A7 chord (other tones tuned previously)
   (All minor chord tones are included in the above)

ACTIVITIES

1. Practice pressing chord bars with eyes closed at first to get the "feel" of the fingering for the I, IV, and V7 chords in various keys.
2. Play songs in various keys executing the proper chords through touch only.
3. Strum major and minor chords for recognition by sound.
4. Devise different strumming styles based on the character of the songs chosen, then try a combination of plucking and strumming.
5. Use Autoharp in combination with recorder, bells and other instruments to create a small ensemble.
6. In a group setting have player strum a tonic (I) chord in any suitable key; then have each person in the group find a note in the chord that he or she can reproduce by humming or singing on a neutral syllable. When player stops strumming, have group sustain the vocal sound to determine the number of different notes of the chord being sung. Vary the activity by having the player strum chord progressions, such as I-IV-I or I-IV-V7-I, with each person singing a note of choice in the initial chord followed by a different note in the succeeding chords.
7. Try accompaniments by ear to songs of choice.

UKULELE

The *ukulele* (or *uke*, as it is often called) is also a chording instrument except that unlike the Autoharp there are no chord bars to press. Chords are *fingered* with the left hand while the right hand does the strumming. (This is sometimes reversed with left-handed individuals.)

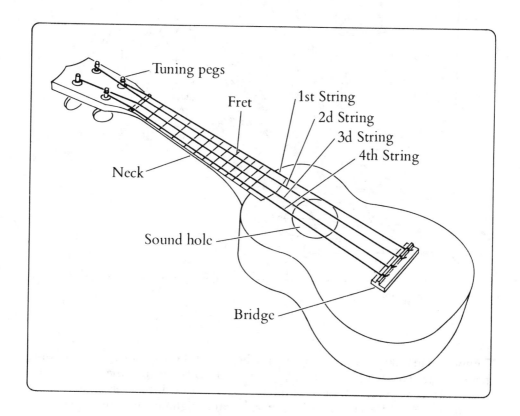

Holding   The uke is held with its neck to the player's left and the body of the uke pressed against the front side of the player's body slightly to the right. The inside of the right forearm is used to steady the instrument so that the right hand will be free for strumming. Strumming may be done with a pick or by using all the fingers on the strumming hand in an up and down motion with lots of flexibility in the wrist.

The fingers of the left hand should curve over the keyboard, with the thumb pressed firmly against the back of the neck of the uke in opposition to the fingers. Space should be left between the neck of the uke and the inside curve of the player's thumb and forefinger.

Tuning   The uke is tuned to the pitches A D F♯ B (shown on following page). Note that strings run 4, 3, 2, 1 from left to right; thus the string closest to the player is the *fourth* string, tuned to A. Use a pitch pipe or similar device for tuning. Sound each string by plucking, then tighten the tuning peg for a higher pitch or loosen it for a lower one. (Stringed instruments require frequent tuning.)

Playing   To play, fingers are placed on the appropriate strings (as indicated by the black dots in the tablature) between the *frets*. Frets are the small metal bands running crosswise on the neck, but the same word is also used to indicate the space *between* the metal bands where the fingers should be placed.

   Chords are fingered according to the given *tablature*. In the chord tablature shown below, the four vertical lines represent the strings of the uke. The black dots indicate where the fingers of the left hand are to be placed.

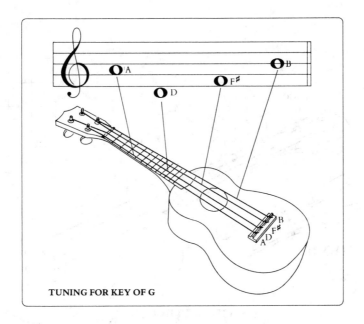

TUNING FOR KEY OF G

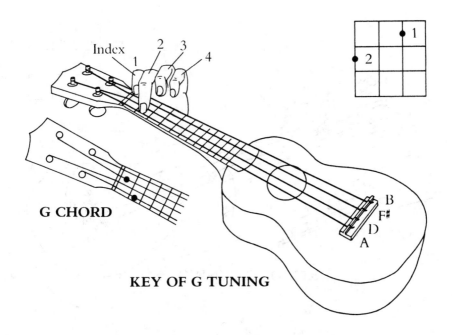

G CHORD

KEY OF G TUNING

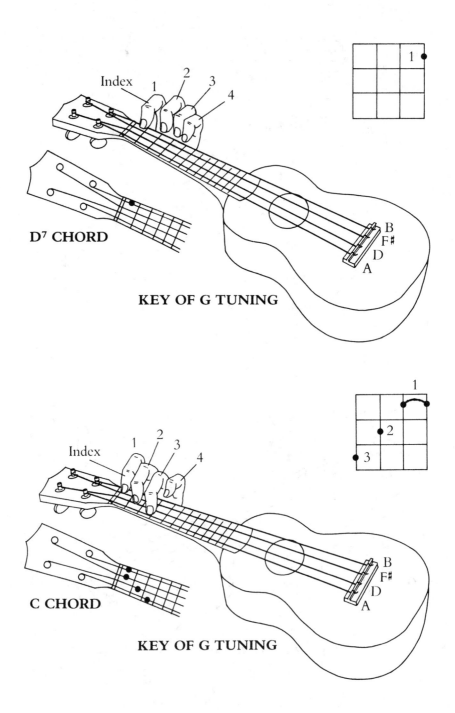

D⁷ CHORD

KEY OF G TUNING

C CHORD

KEY OF G TUNING

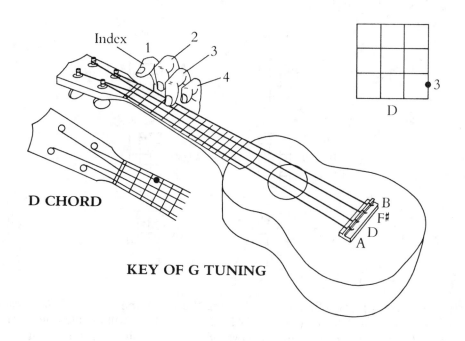

Index 1 2 3 4

D CHORD

KEY OF G TUNING

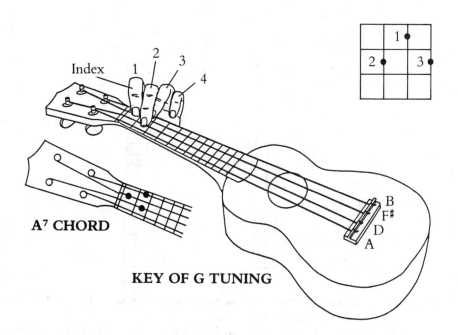

Index 1 2 3 4

A⁷ CHORD

KEY OF G TUNING

The A D F♯ B tuning makes it possible to play the principal chords in the keys of G and D easily:

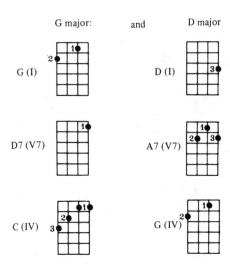

Try songs on pp. 47, 62, and 216 showing the foregoing chords. Tuning each string a whole step lower (from A D F♯ B to G C E A) will enable one to play the I, IV, and V7 chords in the keys of F and C using the same fingering positions as those shown for the keys of G and D.

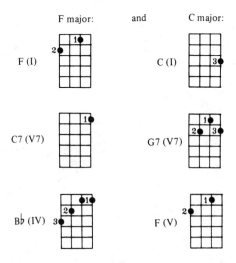

Although it is possible to play these same chords without retuning, the finger positions required are slightly more exotic.

See p. 275 for "Additional Ukulele Chords," then try selected songs in this book.

If finger positions seem too awkward in some keys, transpose chords to a different key to facilitate more comfortable progressions. (See "Transposing Chords," p. 210.)

ADDITIONAL UKULELE CHORDS

All the chords shown below are in the key-of-G tuning (A D F♯ B).

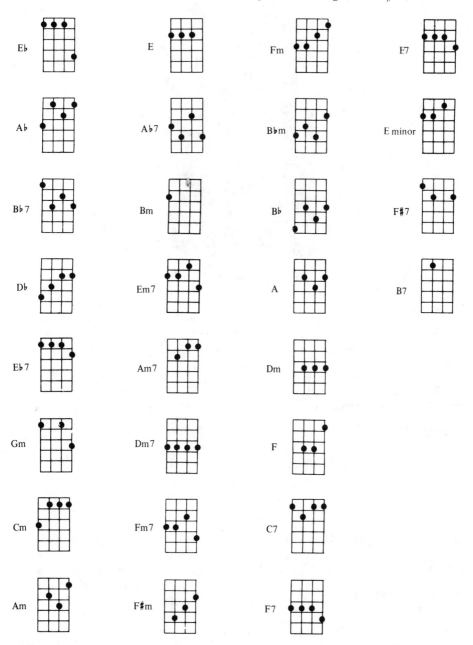

BARITONE UKULELE

For those who find the guitar too large and the uke too small, the baritone ukulele represents a comfortable compromise.

Ukulele   **Baritone Ukulele**

Although the baritone uke has only four strings, they are pitched lower than those of the soprano uke, which, when combined with a slightly larger size, makes the baritone uke sound more like a guitar.

Holding   The baritone uke is held in the same manner as the soprano uke, with slight adjustments in "stretch" for its larger size.

Tuning   Tuning for the baritone uke is from the bass clef:

Playing   The tablature is read in the same way as for the soprano uke; however, because of the different tuning the chords will show different names from those indicated for the soprano uke for the same finger positions. All chord letters are five below those indicated for the same tablature on the soprano uke.

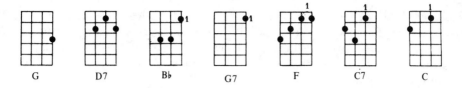

GUITAR

The guitar, like the uke, must also be fingered, but as it has *six* strings, the positions will vary.

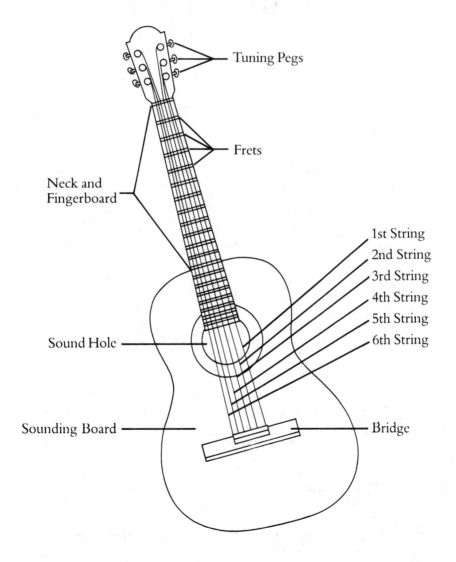

Holding   The guitar is held and played in much the same manner as the ukulele except that because of its larger size, a strap is frequently added to help support the weight. When first learning it is helpful to use a small stool on which to rest the left foot so that it too may support some of the weight of the instrument.

Tuning   The pitches of the strings are changed by tightening or loosening the tuning pegs attached to the strings at the upper part of the instrument. The guitar is tuned as follows:

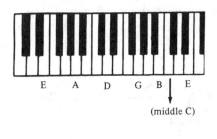

(middle C)

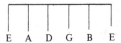

E   A   D   G   B   E

Relative Tuning for Guitar   An alternate method of tuning relies on one string to tune another. Once the pitch of the first or sixth string (high E or low E) is established, various frets are fingered to tune remaining strings.

PRESSING ON THIS STRING:	AT THIS FRET POSITION:	WILL MATCH THE PITCH OF:
2nd	5th	1st string E
3rd	4th	2nd string B
4th	5th	3rd string G
5th	5th	4th string D
6th	5th	5th string A

Playing   Guitar tablature is read in the same way as for the uke. With six strings on the guitar, however, care must be taken at the outset to note when the strings are meant to be played *open* (O), that is, with *no* fingers pressed on them, and when they are not to be played at all (X). The following symbols are used for these conditions:

X = string not played
O = string played open

Strings on the guitar may be plucked as well as strummed, which adds variety and interest to its rhythmic accompaniment.

Guitar Chords

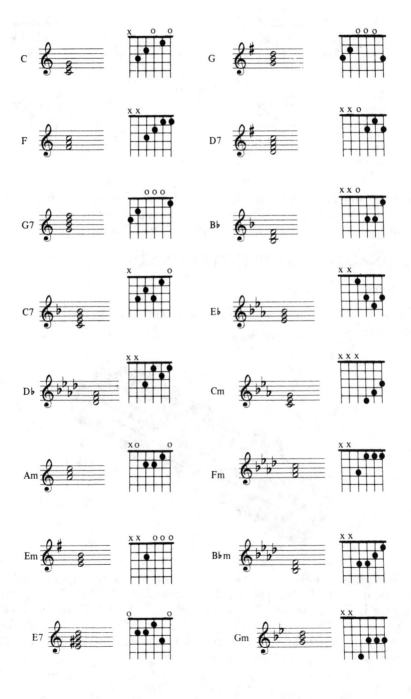

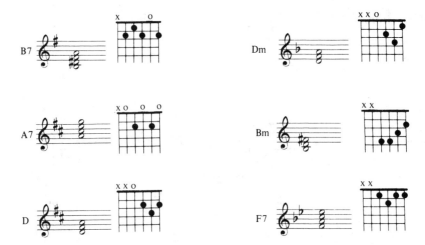

Changing from one key to another can be done through the use of a capo (small attachment for the instrument) or through transposition. (See "Transposition," p. 129, and "Transposing Chords," p. 210.)

OPTIONAL HARMONY INSTRUMENTS

Harmonica

Breathing in and out is about the only skill required for playing a recognizable tune on the harmonica.

As shown in the photo of the harmonica, a number appears over each opening of the instrument. For playing, the harmonica is held so that the number 1 opening is to the player's left. Openings 4, 5, 6, and 7 are the ones used most frequently. Each opening can produce two different sounds, depending on whether the breath is blown or drawn. When reading numbers for a song, a plain number means to blow the breath out:

4 5 6 7
blow

A circled number means to draw the breath in:

④⑤⑥⑦
draw

The numbers are translated into tunes by a combination of blowing and drawing;

4   4   6   6   ⑥   ⑥   6

blow blow blow blow draw draw blow

The foregoing pattern is the first line of "Twinkle, Twinkle Little Star."
Try the following songs from the numbers:

KUM BA YAH

4 5 6 6 6 ⑥⑥ 6
4 5 6 6 6 ⑤ 5 ④
4 5 6 6 6 ⑥⑥ 6
⑤ 5 4 ④④ 4

ROW ROW ROW

4 4 4 ④ 5 5 ④ 5 ⑤ 6
7 7 7 6 6 6 5 5 5 4 4 4
6 ⑤ 5 ④ 4

O SUSANNA

4 ④ 5 6 6 ⑥ 6 5 4 ④ 5 5 ④ 4 ④
4 ④ 5 6 6 ⑥ 6 5 4 ④ 5 5 ④④ 4
4 ④ 5 6 6 ⑥ 6 5 4 ④ 5 5 ④ 4 ④
4 ④ 5 6 6 ⑥ 6 5 4 ④ 5 5 ④④ 4
⑤⑤⑥⑥ 6 6 5 4 ④
4 ④ 5 6 6 ⑥ 6 5 4 ④ 5 5 ④④ 4

MARINE'S HYMN

4 5 6 6 6 6 6 7 6
5 ⑤ 6 6 ⑤④ 4
4 5 6 6 6 6 6 7 6
5 ⑤ 6 6 ⑤④ 4
7 ⑦⑥⑤⑥ 7 6 ⑥ 6
7 ⑦⑥⑤⑥ 7 6
5 ⑤ 6 6 6 6 6 7 6
5 ⑤ 6 6 ⑤④ 4

ARE YOU SLEEPING

4 ④ 5 4 4 ④ 5 4
5 ⑤ 6 5 ⑤ 6
6 ⑥ 6 ⑤ 5 4
6 ⑥ 6 ⑤ 5 4
4 2 4 4 2 4

A major scale may also be played using the four openings:

4 ④ 5 ⑤ 6 ⑥ ⑦ 7
DO RE MI FA SOL LA TI DO

Harmonicas are manufactured in different keys; however, the same playing principles apply to all harmonicas regardless of key. The blow-draw pattern shown above would be the same for a major scale on the harmonica in any key. Only the letter names would differ depending on the key of the harmonica. For purposes of the examples shown below, it should be assumed that a key-of-C harmonica is being used. Playing from notation begins with familiarity with the blow-draw scale pattern:

4 ④ 5 ⑤ 6 ⑥ ⑦ 7
DO RE MI FA SOL LA TI DO

then transferring that knowledge to songs in the key of C, reading directly from notation without using the numbers. (Try songs on pp. 44, 156, 157, 287.) Songs selected for reading from notation will be limited to those written in the key of the harmonica used.

To enable playing a larger repertoire of songs, it is suggested that songs in keys not suitable for the harmonica at hand be transposed to the appropriate key. (See "Transposition," p. 129.)

Chromatic harmonicas allow the playing of chromatic tones as well as tones of the scale.

Chords on Resonator Bells

The use of resonator bells as a *melody* instrument was discussed in Chapter 6. The chord information shown here is intended to enable the use of the bells as a *harmony* instrument as well. Striking the bells indicated will produce the designated chords.

CHORD	BELLS	CHORD	BELLS
C	C E G	G7	G B D F
D	D F♯ A	A7	A C♯ E G
E♭	E♭ G B♭	B♭7	B♭ D F A♭
F	F A C	C7	C E G B♭
G	G B D	D7	D F♯ A C
A♭	A♭ C E♭	E♭7	E♭ G B♭ D♭
A	A C♯ E	D♭	D♭ F A♭
B♭	B♭ D F	F7	F A C E♭

Other selected chords include these:

CHORD	BELLS
a min	A C E
c min	C E♭ G
d min	D F A
g min	G B♭ D
e min	E G B
f min	F A♭ C
B7	B D♯ F♯ A
E7	E G♯ B D

Bottles

Melodies as well as chords may be produced from ordinary soft drink bottles filled with varying amounts of water.

Tuning Bottles may be "tuned" as follows:

A. Press rim of bottle against underside of lower lip, then blow gently across the top, directing the air slightly downward at the same time. The pitch produced by this empty bottle becomes DO (I).

B. Add a small amount of water (½ to 1 inch) to a second bottle and blow gently as suggested in (A.) above to test for the sound of RE. (Add or remove water as needed to secure appropriate pitch.)

C. Fill the remaining six bottles, adding more water to each successive bottle. Test by blowing over the top as before to sound the remaining notes MI FA SOL LA TI and HIGH DO (8). Adding water will raise the pitch, removing water will lower it.

D. If tuning to a specific key is desired, it will be necessary to adjust the water in the DO (I) bottle to the pitch of the keynote and tune the remaining bottles accordingly.

E. Notes below DO (I) require a larger bottle to produce a lower sound. Additional tuned bottles are also needed to play any chromatic tones that occur within a song. (See "Chromatic Tones," p. 162.)

Tunes may be played from syllables or numbers, since each bottle will have been assigned either one or the other at the outset:

ON TOP OF OLD SMOKEY

Syllables:	Numbers:
DO DO MI SOL DO LA	1 1 3 5 8 6
LA FA SOL LA SOL	6 4 5 6 5
SOL DO MI SOL SOL RE	5 1 3 5 5 2
RE MI FA MI RE DO	2 3 4 3 2 1

Chords on Bottles   In addition to tunes, bottles may be used to play chord accompaniment by sounding several bottles simultaneously. Numbers 1–3–5 (DO MI SOL) will sound the I chord, numbers 4–6–8 (FA LA DO) the IV chord and numbers 5–7–2–4 (SOL TI RE FA) the V7 chord. Chords may be sustained under the given melody or varied in style. For "oom-pah" or "oom-pah-pah" accompaniments, use the larger lower-sounding bottles to play the chord root on "oom" and the higher sounding bottles to play the remaining chord notes on the "pahs." If sufficient bottles are available, they may also be used to play the melody over the chordal accompaniment, as well as given parts in songs arranged for two, three, four or more parts.

ACTIVITIES

1. "Tune" eight empty soda bottles of the same size to make up a scale, then select any song within an octave range to play. Add more bottles as necessary to increase song repertoire.

2. Using single bottles in place of voices, play chord roots of selected songs while group sings the song.

3. Select appropriate bottles for chords to accompany various songs, limiting song choice in the beginning to those containing only I, IV, and V7 chords.

4. Try "Chopsticks" (p. 226) using bottles in place of voices on the parts. If desired, add the following chord notes:

    For the two-measure G7 sequence:
      RE SOL throughout.
    For the two-measure C sequence:
      DO SOL throughout.

5. Vary the accompaniment styles, using some sustained, others in "oom-pah" or "pah pah" rhythm.

6. Add other sounds (kazoos, washboard, "gut bucket," etc.) and form a jug band.

Answers to Questions

CHAPTER 1

1. pitch/duration/intensity/timbre
2. pitch
3. intensity
4. timbre
5. an organized series of tones/arrangement of tones in a meaningful sequence.
6. basic pulse/long and short sounds riding over the pulse
7. melody/rhythm/harmony/form
8. form
9. harmony
10. staff/5/4
11. first
12. fourth
13. at the beginning
14. bass clef
15. treble
16. lower
17. bass
18. treble
19. higher
20. higher
21. G
22. E
23. A
24. FACE
25. True
26. A
27. G
28. fifth
29. BED
30. F
31. leger lines
32. A
33. C
34. line/space
35. A/C
36. reverse

37. C
38. C
39. key signature
40. sharps/flats
41. nothing/key signature
42. meter/time signature

CHAPTER 2

1. elements
2. accent
3. even/uneven
4. bar lines/measure
5. end
6. measure
7. meter signature
8. measure
9. two
10. upper figure is 3
11. four beats/measure
12. beginning
13. two
14. $\frac{3}{4}$
15. downward/upward
16. first
17.

18. notes
19. ♩
20. down
21. right
22.

23. 4
24. quarter note
25. $\frac{2}{4}$
26. 3/quarter
27. $\frac{4}{}$ or 𝄴
28. silence

29. note
30. silence
31. 1
32.

a.

b.

c.

33. two
34. two
35. one
36.

a.

b.

c.

d.

37. two
38. ♩/third
39. half
40.

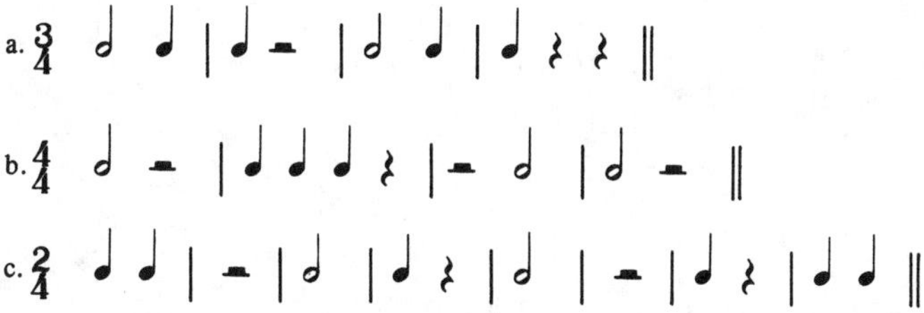

a.

b.

c.

41. different
42. smoothly
43. does not affect
44. three
45. three
46. three
47. ♩.

48.

a. ♩♩♩ | ♩. | ♩ ♩ | ♩. | ♩ ♩ ♩ | ♩. | ♩ ♩ | ♩. ‖

b. ♩♩♩ | ♩. | ♩ ♩♩♩♩ | ♩. ♪ | ♩ ♩ | ♩. ♪ | ♩♩♩♩ | ♩. ♪ ‖

c. ♩. ♪ | ♩♩♩ | ♩ ♩ | ♩♩♩ | ♩. ♪ | ♩. ♪ | ♩ ♩ | ♩♩♩ ‖

49. tie
50. four
51. affects
52. tie/slur/different
53. four
54. stem
55. $\frac{4}{4}$
56. quarter/half
57. silence
58. fourth
59. three
60. False
61. upper figure of the time signature

62.

a. ♩♩ | ♩ | ♩ ♪ | ♩ | ♩ ♪ | ♩♩ | ♪ ♩ ‖

b. ♩. | ♩♩♩ | ♩ ♩ | ♩ ♪ | ♩ ♪ ♩ | ♩. | ♩. ‖

c. ♩. ♩ | ♩ ♪ ♩♩ | ♩ — | ○ ‖

d. ♩ ♩ | — | ♪ — ♩ | ♩. ♩ ‖

63.

a. ♩ or ♪ | ♩ or ♪ | ♩ or ♪ | ‖

b. ♩ or ♪ | | ♩ or — | ♩ or ♪ ‖

c. ♩. | | ♩ or — | ‖

CHAPTER 3

1. faster
2. two
3. one half
4. one
5. half
6. one
7. one and a half
8. two
9. three
10. one half
11. increased/half
12. uneven/even
13. eighth
14. 1½/½
15. two
16.

17. two
18. four
19. four
20. one
21. four
22. quarter
23. eighth
24.

25. uneven
26. quarter/two
27.

a. $\frac{2}{4}$ ♪ ♪♪. ♪| ♫ ♫ | ♬♬ ♬♫ | ♪. ♪♪ ¬ ‖

b. $\frac{3}{4}$ ♩ ♩ ♪. ♪| ♬ ¬ ♪♪. ♪| ¬ ♪♪. ♪♪ | ♪¬ ♩ ♩ ‖

c. $\frac{4}{4}$ ♩ ♫ ♫ ♪. ♪| ♩ ♩ ♫ ♩ | ♩ ♪. ♪♪ ¬ ‖

28. displaced accent
29. first/third
30. syncopated
31. half
32. three/half
33. one
34. ¢
35. four
36. eighth
37. two
38. eighth
39. dotted half
40. simple
41. compound/simple
42. upper
43. two
44. four
45. $\frac{9}{8}$
46. three
47. will not
48. ♪ or ¬ | ♩ or ¬.
    ♩ or ¬. | ♪ or ¬

CHAPTER 4

1. RE
2. TI
3. FA
4. SOL

5.

a.

	DO	RE	MI	FA	SOL	LA	TI	DO
	1	2	3	4	5	6	7	8

6. pitch
7. melody
8. stepwise
9.

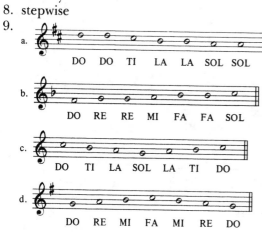

10.

11.

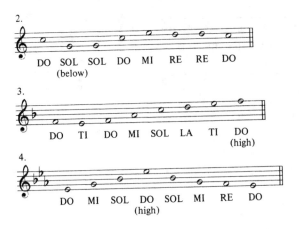

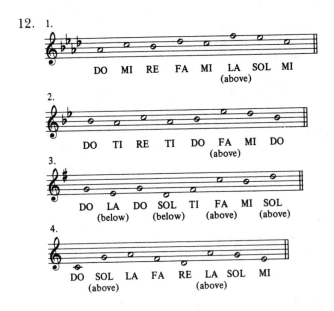

13. short musical thought
14. numerous phrases
15. cadences
16. breath control

CHAPTER 5

1. interval
2. 4th
3. 3rd
4. a. 4th; b. 4th; c. 6th; d. octave

 5. major/DO
 6. 3rd/4th/7th/8th
 7. MI/FA
 8. TI/DO
 9. 88
10. half
11. whole
12. half—E/F and B/C
13. black
14. E–F/B–C
15. C D E F G A B C
16. C
17. sharps/flats
18. interval
19. half
20. half
21.

22. F♯
23. C♯
24. ♯ (sharp)
25. key signature
26. G
27. fifth
28. See "Summary of Scales in Sharp Keys," p. 110–111
29. A/G♯/F♯/E/A
30. B♭
31. B♭
32. F
33. half
34. half
35.

36. A♭/A♭
37. no
38. 3/E♭
39. fourth
40. See "Summary of Scales in Flat Keys," p. 115
41. E♭/G/B♭/A♭/G

42. line
43. above
44. second line
45.

    a.   b.   c.

46. FA
47. next to the last flat
48.

49. 45.

50. DO
51. DO
52. D
53. first line, or fourth space
54. a. Key of B   b. Key of F♯

    c. Key of D

55. D
56. last sharp
57. G
58. F♯
59. second

60.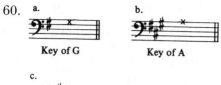

a. Key of G   b. Key of A

c. Key of B

61. space below
62. F
63. F
64. B♭
65. third line
66. first
67. FA
68. 1.

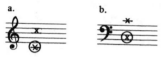

a.   b.

69. 2.

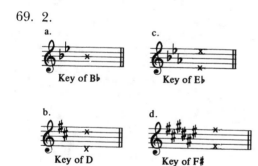

a. Key of B♭   c. Key of E♭

b. Key of D   d. Key of F♯

70. F
71. fifth
72. second
73. third
74. F, C, G
75. high
76. D
77. five
78. third

79. second
80. fourth
81. second/third
82. G
83.

84. four

CHAPTER 7

1. chromatic
2. chromatic
3. ♮ or ♯ or ♭
4. False
5. key
6. ♯ (sharp)
7. lower
8. white
9. ♮ (natural sign)
10. natural
11. True
12. False
13. True
14. True
15. DI
16. RI
17. letter/"ee"
18. True
19. False
20. True
21. cancel/flat
22. ME
23. RAH
24. TI
25. cancel
26. sharp
27. double flat
28. sharped

CHAPTER 8

1. major/minor
2. DO
3. modes

4. LA
5. major
6. LA
7. one
8. different from
9. three
10. melodic
11. harmonic
12. natural
13. d minor
14. key signature
15. one and a half
16. See "Summary of Relative Minor Keys," page 186
17. key signatures
18. starting tone
19. key signatures

CHAPTER 9

1. harmony
2. triad
3. root
4. root/third/fifth
5. five
6. two whole
7. one and a half
8. first
9. tonic
10. IV
11. DO
12. first/fourth/fifth
13. subdominant/dominant
14.

15. four
16. one and a half
17. dominant seventh
18. SOL/V
19.

20. I or tonic

21. V7
22. SOL
23. FA
24. letter names
25. root
26. C
27. F
28. C
29. G7
30. C/G7/C/F/G7/C
31. I/IV/V7/I/V7/I
32. F
33. IV
34. C7
35. F/Bb/F/Bb/C7/F
36. I/V7/I/IV/V7/I
37. D7
38. IV
39. G C D D7
    I IV V V7
40. I/V7/I/IV/V7/I
41. G/D7/G/C/G
42. I/IV/I/V7/I
    G/C/G/D7/G
43. root
44. inversion
45. third
46. second
47. inversions
48. a. root   b. inversion   c. inversion
49. lowering/one-half
50. whole/one and a half
51.

52. 1st/4th/5th
53. D
54. C
55. f minor
56. cadences
57. half
58. comma
59. V7 (or V)/I
60. plagal

61. root syllable
62. I (or tonic)
63. FA
64. V7
65. four
66. one
67. No
68. C
69. FA
70. G/DO
71. G
72. DO FA DO SOL DO
    C   F   C   G7   C
73. vocal chording
74. common tone
75. DO/MI/SOL
76. IV
77. V7
78. DO
79. I/V7 or V
80. FA
81. first soprano/second soprano/alto
82. lower
83. SSAA
84. first tenor
85. first tenor/second tenor/first bass (or baritone)/bass
86. soprano/alto
87. bass
88. soprano/alto/tenor/bass
89. soprano/alto/baritone
90. choirs
91. string
92. violin
93. alto
94. bass viol
95. harp
96. plucking
97. higher
98. blowing
99. piccolo
100. flute/reeds
101. single reed/double reed
102. single
103. oboe
104. contrabassoon
105. brass

106. French horn
107. trombone
108. tuba
109. tightening/loosening
110. percussion
111. kettle drums (tympani)
112. chimes/bells/xylophone/celesta (any two)
113. yes/MI
114. V or V7
115. DO/FA
116. root
117. C
118. IV
119. C
120.

Glossary

Accidental Chromatic sign (♮, ♯, ♭, x, ♭♭) altering the pitch of a given tone within a measure.

Alla breve (¢) Cut time or halved time meaning that $\frac{4}{4}$ meter becomes $\frac{2}{2}$.

Alto The lowest child's or woman's voice; also, a part within a certain range, whether played or sung.

Atonal Without a fixed reference point; no home tone or key.

Band A group of performers or a certain specified group of instruments. String instruments are not usually included in a band.

Bar lines Vertical lines drawn so as to divide a staff into measures.

Bass The lowest male voice; also, a part within a certain range, whether played or sung.

Bass clef (𝄢) First line of the staff bearing this symbol is G.

Cadence Stopping or pausing place in a section of music.

Cancel (♮) A chromatic sign nullifying the effect of any previous sign placed before a note.

Canon A musical form in which a given melody is imitated by other voices beginning at different times.

Chord Three or more tones sounded simultaneously.

Chorus A group of people singing together; also, a composition written for combined voices; also, the part of a song that is repeated after each verse.

Chromatic Tones foreign to a given key or scale; also, all tones of the chromatic scale.

Chromatic scale A twelve-tone scale of half steps within any given octave.

Composer One who writes music.

Concerto A symphonic composition written for solo instrument (or group of instruments) and orchestra, usually consisting of three contrasting movements.

Conductor One who directs a chorus, orchestra, band or any musical group.

Consonance A combination of tones which, when sounded simultaneously, produces a feeling of rest.

Da Capo (D.C.) From the beginning. A direction to repeat the entire piece from the beginning to the place where the word *Fine* appears, or to the end.

Dal Segno (𝄋) A direction to repeat from the sign to the word Fine.

Descant A melody sung or played against the main melody of a song.

Dissonance A combination of tones which, when sounded simultaneously, produces a feeling of tension or unrest.

Dominant Fifth tone of the major scale; also, a chord built on the fifth tone of the major scale.

Dominant seventh Chord built on the dominant (fifth) tone of the scale, consisting of four tones.

Double bar (𝄁) Two vertical bars signifying the end of a section or a whole piece of music.

Duet A musical performance by two voices or instruments.

Duple meter Meter in which there are two beats or some multiple of two in each measure.

Dynamics Varying intensities of sound throughout a given musical composition.

Electronic music Music produced by distorting or modifying various sounds through the process of electronic devices.

Fermata ⌢ See *Hold*.

Fine   The end of a composition.

Flat (♭)   A musical symbol representing a tone one half step below the note before which it is placed.

Folk song   A song, usually of unknown origin, arising as an outgrowth of a people and handed down through generations by oral tradition.

Form   The basic structure of a musical composition, resulting from the arrangement of repetition and contrast in the material.

Fugue   Literally, "flight." A contrapuntal form involving two or more voices in which a subject (theme) is introduced and developed through a series of imitations.

Half step   The interval between two adjacent tones on the keyboard.

Harmony   The sound resulting from the simultaneous sounding of two or more tones consonant with each other.

Hold ⌒   Symbol over a note indicates that the note should be held longer than the given rhythm of the note would ordinarily require. Also called *fermata*.

Imitation   The reproducing of a given melody by several voices at different times.

Instrument   An implement with which musical sounds are produced.

Interval   The pitch distance between two tones.

Inversion   In harmony, the presence of any tone other than the root appearing as the bass note of a chord.

Jazz   A twentieth-century musical style characterized by duple meter, syncopation and improvisation. Considered to be typically American.

Key   Refers to the specific tonality of a musical selection as determined by the keynote and corresponding scale system.

Key note   Home tone/initial tone of any given scale or key. See also *Tonic*.

Key signature   The group of sharps or flats at the beginning of a piece of music indicating the key (or scale) of the music.

Legato   Smooth, flowing. Opposite of *staccato*.

Measure   A measured space on the staff enclosed between two bar lines.

Melody   An arrangement of single tones in a meaningful sequence.

Meter   A specified arrangement of beats within a measure.

Meter signature   A set of two numbers at the beginning of music, the upper figure determining the number of beats in each measure and the lower figure determining the kind of note that will receive one beat. Some examples are $\frac{3}{4}$, $\frac{2}{2}$, $\frac{6}{8}$.

Minor   Mode in which LA is the tonal center or keynote.

Mixed chorus   A group of male and female singers performing together.

Mode   A specified arrangement of scale tones.

Natural   See *Cancel*.

Orchestra   A group of instrumental performers or a certain specified group of instruments.

Ostinato   A repeated melodic or rhythmic fragment.

Overture   An instrumental selection which is usually performed before the curtain rises on a musical play, and which contains tunes that will be heard later in the production. *Concert overtures* may also be performed as independent pieces.

Pentatonic scale   Five-tone scale consisting of the tones DO RE MI SOL LA.

Phrase   A small section of a composition comprising a musical thought. May be compared to a sentence in language.

Pitch   The highness or lowness of a tone, determined by the frequency of vibration of sound waves. The greater the number of vibrations, the higher the resulting pitch.

Polyphony   Literally "many voices." The combining of a number of individual harmonizing melodies. *Polyphonic music* — refers to music in which two or more melodies sound simultaneously.

Polyrhythms   Two or more contrasting rhythms sounded simultaneously.

Polytonal music   Music in which two or more keys are sounded simultaneously.

Quartet   A musical group of four voices or instruments; also, a composition written for four parts (voices or instruments).

Rhythm   Measured motion; the regular recurrence of accent; the pattern of long and short sounds within a series of tones.

Rondo   An instrumental form in which a recurring main theme (A) alternates with two or more secondary themes (B and C).

Root   The tone of the scale upon which a chord is built.

Root position   The position of a chord in which the root appears as the lowest tone.

Round   A form of imitative singing in which voices enter at measured time intervals and sing the melody as many times as desired.

Scale   A graduated series of tones arranged in a specified order. From the Italian word *scala*, meaning "ladder."

Sharp (♯) Musical symbol representing a tone one half step above the tone before which it is placed.

Slur A curved line drawn between two or more notes of different pitches, indicating that they are to be executed in a smoothly connected manner:

Solo A musical performance by one voice or instrument.

Soprano Highest treble voice; also, a part within a certain range, whether played by an instrument or sung.

Staccato Sounded in a short, detached manner. Literally, "separate."

Staff Five equally spaced horizontal lines and four spaces upon which music is written.

Subdominant Fourth tone of the scale (FA); chord built on the fourth tone of the scale.

Subject The principal theme on which a musical composition is based.

Suite An instrumental form that may consist of a group of dances, a group of descriptive pieces, or a group of pieces from a ballet or opera, unified through a story or idea.

Symphony A large musical work in sonata form for full orchestra.

Syncopation The rhythmic result of a normally accented beat being displaced onto an unaccented beat.

Tempo The rate of speed at which a musical composition is performed.

Tenor The highest male voice; also, a part within a certain range, whether played by an instrument or sung.

Theme A short musical passage that states an idea, often providing the basis for variations or development in a musical composition.

Tie A curved line connecting two or more notes of the same pitch, indicating that the first note is to be held for the duration of the combined beats of all the others appearing in the tie:

Timbre The quality of a musical tone that distinguishes voices and instruments.

Time signature See *Meter signature*.

Tonal music Music in a definite key; having a key tone or home tone.

Tonality The feeling of the presence of and tendency to be drawn toward a certain home tone or key in a piece of music.

Tone A musical sound; the quality of a musical sound.

Tonic Keynote of a given key; chord built on tonic note of the scale.

Transpose To transfer a musical composition from one key into another.

Treble clef 𝄞 First line of the staff bearing this symbol is E.

Trio A musical group of three voices or instruments; also, a composition written for three parts (voices or instruments).

Triple meter Meter in which there are three beats or some multiple of three to the measure.

Triplet Three notes performed in the time of two of the same value. ♪♪♪, ♩♩♩ etc.

Variations Different treatments of a given theme or melody through changes in rhythm, mood, tempo, meter, etc.

Whole step The sum of intervals of two adjacent half steps.

Whole-tone scale A scale of six tones in which all intervals are whole steps.

See pp. 75 and 76 for additional musical terms and symbols related to tempo, dynamics and expression.

Summary of Musical Symbols

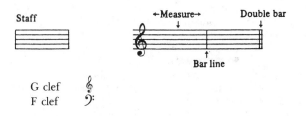

Staff   ←Measure→   Double bar

Bar line

G clef
F clef

LINES AND SPACES

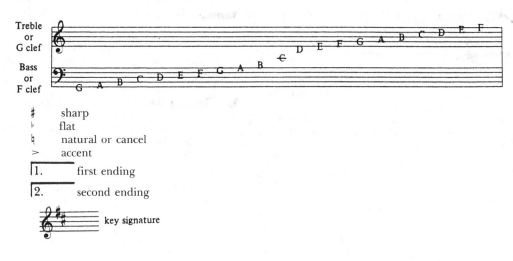

Treble
or
G clef

Bass
or
F clef

♯   sharp
♭   flat
♮   natural or cancel
>   accent

|1.   first ending

|2.   second ending

key signature

leger lines

$\frac{2}{4}$	meter signature
$\mathcal{C}$	cut time
c $\frac{4}{4}$	time
:‖	repeat
⌒	hold or *fermata*
D. C.	Go back to beginning. End at *Fine*.
D. S.	Go back to sign 𝄋. End at *Fine*.
Fine	End.

NOTES

Quarter note	♩
Half note	♩
Dotted half note	♩.
Whole note	𝅝
Eighth notes	♫ ♪ ♪
Sixteenth notes	♬ ♪ ♪ ♪ ♪
Dotted quarter note	♩.
Dotted eighth note	♪.
Triplet	(3)♬ (3)♩ ♩ ♩

RESTS

Quarter rest	𝄽
Half rest	𝄼
Whole rest	𝄻
Eighth rest	𝄾
Sixteenth rest	𝄿

General Index

Song Index